Indians of the Great Basin and Plateau

Among the most interesting Indian tribes in the United States are those of the Columbia Plateau and the Great Basin. Author Francis Haines tells the exciting stories of the Nez Perce, Flatheads, and Shoshoni from earliest times to the present day. The Nez Perce are noted for their friendship with the Lewis and Clark Expedition, and later they waged a spectacular war against the United States. The Flatheads, who asked the whites for missionaries, held the Montana passes against the Blackfeet. The Shoshoni, who held lands across the main routes of Western travel, helped introduce horses to the Northwest.

WILLIAM K. POWERS

Consulting Editor

AMERICAN INDIANS THEN AND NOW

Indians OF THE Great Basin AND Plateau

Francis Haines

An American Indians Then & Now Book

Earl Schenck Miers, General Editor

G. P. Putnam's Sons New York

Contents

Indians of the Great Basin
and Plateau

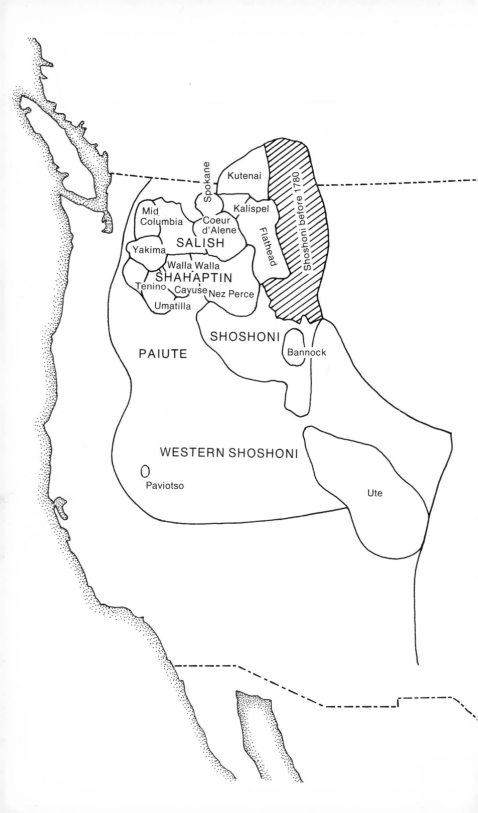

1 Of Man and Salmon

PRIMITIVE MAN, like more recent pioneers, usually tried to find a home for himself where he had the best chance of survival. He sought soil which would produce vegetable foods, land where there was game and fish, wood for shelter and fuel.

On the North American continent few areas are more hostile to man than what is called the Great Basin and the Plateau of the present-day Western United States. This vast, high, rough, arid region is bounded on the west by the Cascade-Sierra Nevada mountain ranges and on the east by the Continental Divide.

The Great Basin proper, about half the entire area, is so named because it has no drainage to the ocean. Completely surrounded by mountains, the floor of the basin is high desert broken by rough ranges. Its southern rim is the drainage divide of the Colorado River system extending from southeastern California across Nevada and half of Utah. Eastern Utah, western Colorado, and a portion of southwestern Wyoming are customarily included as part of the Great Basin culture area.

The northern rim of the Great Basin is the divide separating it from the Columbia River drainage. The entire Columbia drainage east of the Cascades and south of the Canadian border is called the Plateau. This whole area—both Great Basin and Plateau—is a hostile land of high desert, jagged mountains, and deep canyons. Only among the foothills of the encircling mountain ranges and in some of the river valleys could primitive man live with any certainty of food and shelter.

This huge area supported a scanty population, possibly 53,000 people, when the first white men entered its forbidding fastness at the end of the eighteenth century. Well over half this total was concentrated along some 200 miles of the Columbia River in present-day central Washington, crowded between the rushing waters and the cliffs towering against the sky.

The climate of the Columbia Basin is modified by the high wall of the Cascade Range to the West, protecting the land from storms sweeping off the Pacific Ocean. The warm, moist air masses are carried off the ocean by the prevailing westerlies and dump large amounts as rain or snow. As the air masses slide down the eastern slopes, they are relatively dry and pick up moisture from the

10

Indians net salmon jumping the rapids on the Columbia River.
(Copyright, 1899, Oregon Historical Society, Portland, Oregon)

land, leaving it a desert. It is windy country where sand particles sting your skin, where fierce blizzards howl in winter.

This bleak land along the rivers lacked vegetable foods, timber for buildings, even wood for fires. Game animals and birds were very scarce. But for primitive man it had one great resource that outweighed all its deficiencies.

It had salmon in hordes—sockeyes, humpbacks, silver cohos, and above all, the lordly chinook, the king salmon. These fish came up from the ocean each year in

11

uncounted millions, seeking the gravel spawning beds high in the mountains at the heads of the smaller streams. At the mouth of each tributary stream a portion of the horde left the river, until by August the most ambitious had penetrated even to the farthest reach of the Salmon River high in the mountains of central Idaho. On the gravel beds they spawned and died, leaving the young salmon to make their way in due time down to the ocean, where they in turn would grow to adult size and return each to its own little stream to repeat the cycle.

Along the rivers, rock slides from the cliffs or boulders swept down from some steep side canyon in time of flood piled up in the riverbeds, damming the current and forming rapids. Rock dikes across the riverbeds also created rapids and small falls. Usually at the foot of each rapid was an eddy, a backwater, where the salmon could rest before tackling the fresh obstacle. By each eddy, at each rapid, and particularly at each side stream, the Indians waited with harpoons, spears, and nets, harvesting food for the coming year.

2 Tribes of the Columbia Basin

THOUSANDS OF YEARS ago several small groups of Indians moved from the Pacific coast up the Columbia River, pushed out by powerful neighbors from the lower country. Their movement was slow and may have come in several waves over a period of hundreds of years.

The several bands moving up the river were all of a common language stock, the Shahaptin. In the course of time they held both banks of the Columbia from the mouth of the John Day River to the rapids above the mouth of the Yakima River. On the Oregon side were the Tenino, Umatilla, Cayuse, and Wallawalla, while the Washington side was occupied by the Klikitat, Yakima, and Wanapum. Most of these Indians lived in the valleys of the tributary streams, rather than on the

13

banks of the Columbia. The Palouse tribe held both banks of the Snake River for about 60 miles from the mouth of the stream, with their main villages on the north bank.

The Nez Perce, historically the most important of all the Shahaptins, held the Snake River from the Palouse country up to the mouth of Hell's Canyon, all the Clearwater drainage, and the Salmon River from its mouth to a point about 50 miles above the mouth of the Little Salmon.

All the northern part of the Columbia Basin was held by the Salish-speaking tribes who came across the Cascades from the vicinity of Puget Sound. Once across the mountains, they moved down the Columbia until they were stopped by the Wanapum and Yakima. They spread upriver, occupying the whole drainage to the headwaters in British Columbia and Montana, and some crossed the mountains into the buffalo country.

The Salish tribes included the Mid-Columbia, Wenatchee, Okanogan, Nespelem, Colville, Sanpoil, and Spokane, all in Washington; the Kalispel and Coeur d'Alene in northern Idaho; the Flatheads in western Montana and across Marias Pass to the edge of the plains in northern Montana. While the Kutenai lived just north of the border in British Columbia and across Crowsnest Pass into Alberta and were of a related language group, they are included with the Salish because of their close association with the Kalispel and Flatheads and their common enmity against the Blackfeet.

Although the Shahaptin and Salish languages were

Mounted Nez Perce warriors, photographed by Major Lee Moorhouse, July 4, 1906.

(The Smithsonian Institution)

different, there was no great antagonism between the various villages of the two groups. Always there was a little trade and some visiting back and forth, and there developed a common culture which ignored the language divisions, although each tribe had its local variations in the common pattern. For thousands of years as recent explorations of ancient village sites have shown, the fisherfolk lived in their little villages, their entire lives centered on the annual run of salmon.

15

On several of the rivers, sheer falls formed impassable barriers to the salmon, preventing any of these fish from reaching the upper valleys. Kettle Falls on the Columbia, Spokane Falls on the Spokane, and Salmon Fishing Falls on the Snake marked the upper limits of the salmon run on those streams. Any tribes venturing above those falls had to adjust to a different food supply, a scantier and more varied diet.

The Kalispel on Pend Oreille Lake and the Coeur d'Alene on Coeur d'Alene Lake had fairly large supplies of fresh fish from these two lakes. Before they had horses, they traded with the Spokane villages below the falls, but it is unlikely that they carried any substantial supplies of salmon home.

Both the Kutenai and the Flatheads were too far away from the fisheries even to visit in substantial numbers until they secured horses and could travel the rough country on horseback. The rivers were too swift to allow much use of dugout canoes. These two tribes had some fish in their lakes and rivers, but for the most part they relied on game for their principal food supply. In addition to the deer, elk, mountain sheep, and some moose in the wooded country, they moved out onto the Great Plains east of the mountains to hunt buffalo. They supplemented their game with several kinds of berries and roots. Their hunting and food gathering made them more active and adventurous than the people in the fishing villages along the Columbia.

Among the Shahaptin tribes, the historically important Nez Perce had a good run of salmon in their rivers,

16

but at their fishing places it was difficult to catch enough fish during the run to last the village until the next year. Although fish supplied about 80 percent of their total food, they had to hunt a good deal for game animals and had to put up supplies of roots and berries each summer to carry them through the winter months. But if they worked and made intelligent use of their resources, they could live quite well, even if they did have to put in many more days securing food than did the fishermen farther down the river, where a year's supply could be caught by one man in two or three weeks. Perhaps this demand for intelligent work on the part of the Nez Perce and the resulting varied diet help explain the subsequent behavior of this tribe and its importance in Columbia Basin history.

Throughout the Columbia Basin, side canyons brought down sand and gravel in the spring floods, and alluvial fans were formed along the rivers. These fans were well drained, and the sandy soil was easy to excavate with primitive tools. The little stream from the side canyon furnished cool water in the summer, and the spring floods on the river brought down logs and driftwood for the lodge frames and the cooking fires. Usually the larger rocks from the side canyon formed a small barrier in the river, with a rapid and a pool below for a fishing place. If the side stream was large enough for the spawning salmon to ascend, then it, too, was a fine fishing place. Such alluvial fans furnished the kind of location the Nez Perce liked for their many small villages.

17

During the early period the Nez Perce had from forty to sixty small villages scattered along the Snake, lower Salmon, and Clearwater rivers, each containing about fifty people. The number of people in each village was strictly limited by the available food supply; it was made up of three or four middle-aged couples, perhaps one widow, their married sons with their families, and any unmarried children of the older people. Daughters always married outside the village and lived with their husband's people.

Among the few older men, one would be looked up to as a leader and a person who could give good advice, but he had no power or authority over the rest of the people and could not be called a chief. Nor would one of his teen-age granddaughters, in a group of five or six village girls, rate any such title as Princess. About the middle of the nineteenth century the white men induced the Nez Perce to call some of their leaders Chief, and in the twentieth century they taught the Indians to choose queens and princesses for various celebrations.

Each Nez Perce village owned a great deal of community property, including the village site, the surrounding land for several miles, the fishing places, and the lodges. Personal property consisted of clothes, tools, and weapons for the men, while each woman owned her clothes, some baskets, bags, skins, robes, reed mats, a few skinning knives of stone, a digging stick, and the like.

All the villagers, except the unmarried young men and older boys, lived in a large lodge constructed by

Nez Perce woman and children outside a skin tipi. They hold corn-husk bags and doll cradleboard. Photographed in 1892.

community effort. In earlier times the lodge was circular, with supporting posts for the roof around the edge and near the center. By historic times this lodge had been replaced by a rectangular structure with a center ridge-pole. The strong framework was made of logs. This was supported by short posts at the sides and by a row of tall posts along the middle. Rafters extended from the ridgepole to each side. The whole structure was covered with reed mats, usually in two layers and overlapping to shed the rain. Each woman owned the mats covering the portion of the lodge occupied by her family.

19

A smaller bachelor lodge furnished sleeping quarters for the young men and boys. It was an underground affair with a flat roof only slightly raised above the surface of the ground. A similar small lodge on the other side of the main lodge was a place of refuge for the women, especially when the babies were born. A small hemispherical lodge by the stream was used by the whole village for sweat baths.

To these people the acquiring of enough food was always a big problem, and they all worked to solve it. Once the fishing season was over, the men hunted a good deal, while the women spent much of their time gathering and storing various roots and berries.

Although the valleys of the Clearwater, Salmon, and Snake rivers were nearly as hot and dry in summer as the Columbia Valley to the west, the people could find relief during the summer by climbing to the surface of the adjacent plateau, 2,000 to 3,000 feet above the river. There rain and snow supplied the moisture needed for good pasturelands, shrubs of many kinds, and large forests of pine and fir. Hundreds of species of plants grew in profusion, and the Indians in time learned the food values of each.

The women gathered the roots of the kouse and bitterroot, the bulbs of the camas, currants, huckleberries, serviceberries, rose haws, black moss from the pines (the light gray-green moss from the fir trees is not fit for food), and the stems of the mountain sunflower. The men hunted waterfowl along the streams, grouse on the uplands, antelope on the plains, deer and elk in the meadows and among the brush, mountain sheep and goats among the crags, and both the black bear and the powerful grizzly in the ravines and thickets.

The women wove mats for their houses from the stems of tule and cattail, strong bags from the bast fiber of the Indian hemp, and tight baskets from cedar roots. The men made knives, arrow- and spearpoints, scrapers, and similar tools of chipped and flaked agate, jasper and obsidian. Mountain sheep horns were steamed until soft, then scraped and shaped into dippers, bowls, drinking horns, and spoons. Split into long, narrow strips, the horns could be used to form beautiful bows, the laminated strips held together with fish glue. A few rather clumsy dugout canoes were fashioned from cedar and pine logs and were used in fishing and in crossing the rivers.

The many small Nez Perce villages were united only by bonds of a common language, a common culture, and constant intermarrying. There was no semblance of a tribal organization of any sort. Their closest approach to a larger unity came from the friendly gatherings at the camas grounds each summer.

The camas plant is a member of the lily family, with a starchy bulb and a pretty blue flower which opens in early June. It grows best in open grassland so flat that the drainage is poor and water stands a few inches deep until mid June. After the blossoms wither, the camas plant stores a supply of starch in the bulb for the next year. Then the stem and leaves wither, leaving the seed pod with small, shiny dark seeds, telling the Indian

21

women that the bulbs are now ready for harvest. The Indian women come with their dibbles—the digging sticks—and pile up great mounds of bulbs for cooking and drying before they are put into storage.

At the end of June the snow-fed rivers receded, the salmon run ended, and the hot sun poured into the deep, narrow valleys. When the news came that the camas was ready for harvesting on the cool plateau, all the people were happy to take the reed mats off their houses, leaving the bare framework standing and the entire interior open to the direct rays of the summer sun. When they returned from the camas grounds in September, the floors would be sunbaked, dry, and sterile, ready for another winter's use.

The light, bulky rolls of mats made up most of the loads to be carried up the long, steep climb to the plateau, but they also carried a few sleeping robes, the digging tools, and a small supply of smoked fish. On the return trip, the loads of camas might take two or three trips for each person, before it all could be brought down to the village.

There were three important camas grounds in present-day Idaho for the Nez Perce: one on Camas Prairie near Grangeville; one in the meadows at Weippe; and the third 25 miles north of the Clearwater near Moscow, although this last one may have been occupied by the rather hostile Coeur d'Alene until about 1750. It was clearly in Nez Perce possession by the nineteenth century.

The people from a village usually went to the same

A contemporary scene of Indians fishing at Celilo Falls.
(Geoffrey Hilton)

camp year after year, although there may have been a few young men who would go to another camp for a short time. Even before these people had horses, the people from several villages would gather at each place, forming a camp of 300 or 400 people. Each summer they stayed about six weeks, harvesting, cooking, and baking the camas for winter storage. About half the crop was kept in the form of dried cooked bulbs. The other half was pounded fine after the first cooking, then molded into small cakes and baked quite hard. In this form the camas would keep for months without spoiling as long as it remained dry.

While the camas was cooking in the great pits, the women and children harvested baskets of huckleberries. These could be pressed into cakes and dried in the sun for winter use. A pot of camas mush, flavored with a cake or two of huckleberries, made a tasty dish in the wintertime.

The men guarded the camp against any possible enemies, helped bring in the great piles of wood needed for the fire pits, and hunted game for miles around. They had plenty of time to sit around in the shade and work on tools and weapons or just visit.

This summer camp offered much gaiety for the young people. There they met others of their own age from many villages, people eligible for them to marry, for it was a firm rule that a girl must marry outside her own village and go live with her husband's people.

The women had a pleasant time. They worked together, helping one another, and sisters who had married into different villages could renew family ties. Grandmothers visited with their married daughters and their grandchildren.

The men of the camp held many informal councils around the evening fires, discussing common problems. They could do a little trading of weapons or raw materials, such as good chipping rock. By joining in these activities, the Nez Perce could feel that they all belonged to the same large group, even though they had no formal organization.

Along the Columbia River the good fishing places were few in number, but at each of these, many thousands of salmon could be caught each season. With this more ample food supply, the villages were much larger than those of the Nez Perce, with several hundred people in each. Such a village had to have more organization, more regulation of the village life. There the headmen had such power and authority that they could be considered real chiefs. At the same time they had nothing to compare with the assembling of the Nez Perce at the camas grounds. Although many people would come into a good fishing village to trade, they would not be taken into the village life. Also, in these larger villages there was little interest in marrying the girls off to young men in other villages.

The chief fishing and trading site in northeastern Washington was just below the falls on the Spokane River at the mouth of the Little Spokane. Here people from several tribes came each year to trade and visit. Until the Basin tribes secured horses, all these visitors were neighboring Salish or the related Kutenai. Coeur d'Alene and Kalispel could come rather easily from their villages 30 to 70 miles away. Smaller groups sometimes came from the Kutenai and Flatheads, traveling well over 100 miles cross-country. Since each of these tribes—the Spokane, Coeur d'Alene, Kalispel, Flatheads, and Kutenai—had a well-knit body of several hundred people, they had no inclination to unite into a larger group.

3 The Snake River Country

THE SOUTHERN portion of the Plateau is wholly within the drainage basin of the Snake River above Hell's Canyon. Here the surface of the lava flows slopes gently from an elevation of 6,000 feet near the Wyoming border to about 3,000 feet along the Idaho-Oregon border. Much of the surface of the flow has been but lightly touched by the erosion of a few million years, and the black rock lies exposed to the desert sun over much of the area. Where a thin layer of soil has accumulated, artemisia, rabbit brush, and cactus grow, with a little bunchgrass here and there.

The Snake River rises in the mountains of Wyoming against the Continental Divide and flows in a wide arc westward across the lava, where it has cut a deep box

26

Two women of the Umatilla tribe outside mat-covered tipi. Photographer and date not recorded, but possibly made by Major Lee Moorhouse around 1900.

canyon for 100 miles, dropping in turn over Twin Falls, Shoshoni Falls, and Salmon Fishing Falls. The last falls was thus named because it forms an impassable barrier to the migrating salmon and marks the upper limit of the salmon run. Downstream from the falls the Snake flows for 250 miles through a shallow valley replete with sandhills. During this run it is joined on the left by the Bruneau, the Owyhee, and the Malheur rivers; on the right it receives the Wood, Boise, Payette, and Weiser rivers.

27

For primitive man this upper basin offers two areas where living is possible, but scarcely adequate. Along the lower river, far from the ocean, a run of worn-out salmon comes each year. They are easy to catch, but they are food attractive only to very hungry people. There is little supplementary food to be found in the desert scrub on the plateaus. The camas meadows are small and few. Antelope, jackrabbits, and ground squirrels are scarce. A few deer range on the wooded mountains far to the north.

Once the 5,000-foot level is reached in the upper valley to the east, rainfall becomes more abundant, and the desert scrub gives way to range grasses, with some timber on the northern slopes. This high pasture had a good supply of deer, antelope and elk, while herds of buffalo from time to time drifted south from Montana, although there is some question whether buffalo appeared in the valley in significant numbers before 1700. The salmon run did not reach within 200 miles of this area, but the many small streams which form the headwater drainage of the Snake River and the main river had quantities of freshwater fish.

Although the Columbia Basin was well protected by natural barriers against the invasion of new tribes, the upper Snake River country lay wide open to such invasions. The valley was athwart a natural migration path leading from northern Canada to the southwestern United States. Tribes crossing from Siberia into Alaska followed the Yukon Valley to its head, crossed a rather easy divide, and worked their way southward through

28

the timbered country on the eastern slopes of the mountains. About 200 miles of forest travel brought them out on the open rangelands of the northern Great Plains, the buffalo country. Some of the migrating bands then turned southeast in Montana and kept east of the Rockies on their way south, but other bands kept close to the eastern face of the Rockies, easily passing through the small foothills. When they reached the Missouri River west of Great Falls, they followed up the stream to Three Forks, then up either the Madison or Jefferson fork to the headwaters. Here easy passes led them south into southeastern Idaho and the upper Snake country.

They followed the Snake River down until it turned north on the western border of Idaho. Then the migrants headed south up one of the several small streams flowing from the Owyhee Mountains and crossed a western shoulder of that range. Here at a natural camping site halfway up the mountain from the desert to the west they rested for some time, perhaps many years. They left stone artifacts of many kinds: tools, knives, and projectile points. A recent collection of such artifacts from this campsite can easily be separated into six culture groups, each differing markedly from all the others in pattern and in flaking techniques. Each culture pattern shows a strong preference for a certain kind of rock found in the area, but no two groups used the same kind of rock.

Some of these artifacts from the Owyhee match rather closely artifacts found in southern Arizona along the Gila River, indicating that the migrants who camped

29

on this mountain meadow later moved south to a warmer climate. As each succeeding group moved south, the land was left empty for new arrivals. The Shoshoni of historic times were the last of the migrant groups, arriving in the Owyhee area possibly 1,000 years ago. This pattern is in sharp contrast with that of the Salish and Shahaptin villages in the Columbia Basin, which sometimes show a continuous occupancy of several thousand years, with no culture break to indicate an invasion of new people, and so far there has been no culture earlier than the Shahaptin uncovered in the Columbia Basin.

The Shoshoni belonged to the Ute-Aztecan language group, as did their neighbors, the Bannock, Paiute, Ute, and Paviotso. About 300 years ago the Shoshoni and Bannock held land from the Bow River in Alberta, Canada, south through Montana and Idaho as far as the Great Salt Lake in Utah. By 1800 the Blackfeet, armed with guns by the Hudson's Bay Company traders, had driven the Shoshoni south until they had given up all their Alberta and Montana holdings, although they did venture from time to time into the headwaters of the Missouri to hunt buffalo. This rather recent dispossession of this tribe by the aggressive Blackfeet is often overlooked in historic accounts of the area.

The Shoshoni and Bannock had a fairly adequate food supply as long as they were able to hunt buffalo in southwestern Montana. After they had been driven south into Idaho, they often went hungry and, in general, lived more poorly than did the Salish and Shahaptin tribes in the Columbia Basin. A great deal of their

30

Old woman of the Cayuse tribe weaving a decorated bag. Photo by Major Lee Moorhouse around 1900.

(Smithsonian Institution)

failure to make better use of their food resources could be blamed on the recurring attacks of the more numerous and warlike Blackfeet.

Down the Snake River to the west, below the box canyon and the falls, a few Shoshoni villages were scattered along the river banks for 200 miles downstream. None of the Shoshoni tried to live in the rugged Hell's Canyon beyond that point. The best village sites along the Snake River were at the mouths of the several tributary streams. The salmon there were of poor quality from their long swim from the ocean and were hard to catch in such large rivers, with no falls to form a natural fishing place. This poor-quality fish supplied about half the total food for these people. It was supplemented by seeds, berries, and game, including such items as snakes, lizards, and grasshoppers. These Shoshoni existed barely above the subsistence level. Any small decrease in the food supply brought them to the brink of starvation.

In their villages these Indians had small wickiups covered with grass or reed mats, but when they wandered in search of food, they cached the mats and their larger stone tools and at night sought shelter in a small gully or in the lee of the rimrock. At times they were reduced to building a small, crescent-shaped windbreak of desert scrub about three feet high to break the force of the wind sweeping across the Plateau.

4 The Great Basin

IN THE GREAT BASIN, that vast desert area, there was little food for primitive man. The wide, flat valleys lie at an elevation of 4,000 feet or more, with narrow, jagged mountain ranges rising a mile or so above the valley floor. Patches of timber grow on some of the ranges, usually on the lower northern slopes.

The Great Basin is a complex of several smaller basins, each with a sink or lake at the lowest point. The largest of the basins is drained by the Humboldt River, which winds its way from Nevada's northeastern corner south and west nearly to the California border. For all its length and the large area it drains, the Humboldt carries only a small flow of water. Other Basin streams empty into the Great Salt Lake, Sevier Lake, Walker

Lake, Pyramid Lake, and Carson Sink. In addition to these larger streams, there are many small mountain streams which never reach one of the sinks, but disappear gradually into their alluvial fans. A number of springs, usually in a canyon near the base of a mountain, supply water most of the year. From October to April drinking water may be found here and there over most of the Basin, but during the summer months there are vast stretches with no trace of surface water.

This arid land could support no permanent villages, for there was no spot with an adequate food supply throughout the year. The desert wastes were thinly occupied by an Indian population of possibly 5,000, all belonging to the Ute-Aztecan language group, the latecomers from Asia. These were the Paiute, Gosiute, Paviotso, Washoe, and Western Shoshoni. They roamed the land in small hunting groups, moving nearly every day, gathering berries, seeds, nuts, roots, bulbs, squirrels, rodents, rabbits, snakes, lizards, mice, grasshoppers, Mormon crickets, and the like. Once in a great while they might hope to kill a deer or an antelope. Because of their continual search for edible roots and bulbs, they were known to the early white visitors as Diggers. For several months of each year they were close to starvation. During the good months at best they had only a scanty subsistence diet. Each hunting group usually consisted of about eight to fifteen persons, one or two men, their wives and children. A large group could not find sufficient food in one place.

These people had very few possessions, only what

34

A Paiute woman gathering seed. Photo taken in the valley of the Mospa, southern Nevada, by John K. Hillers of the Powell Expedition, 1871–1875.

(Smithsonian Institution)

they could carry on their travels. They built small wicki-ups for shelter in stormy weather, covering the framework with a few mats and some grass. During the winter they sometimes erected more substantial wicki-ups, where they took shelter from the storms, and wandered widely during better weather. Their grinding stones were left at each campsite where they might expect to find seeds.

5 The Ute

East of the Great Basin, but included as part of the same culture area, is the upper drainage of the Colorado River from the Uinta Mountains on the north to the Continental Divide on the east, and the Junction of the Green River with the Colorado on the south. To the west the rugged mountains of Central Utah form the divide between the Colorado drainage and the Great Basin proper. The valleys of the Green and the upper Colorado had more natural food than did the Great Basin; except for the lack of buffalo, the land was similar to the upper Snake country. The rainfall on the western slopes of the Rockies is adequate to support good grasslands and much timber on the higher slopes. Along the rivers vegetables and fruit could be grown on

36

A Ute hut with corn drying outside. Photo taken in the Unita Valley, on the eastern slope of the Wasatch Mountains, Utah, by John K. Hillers, of the Powell Expedition, 1871–1875.

(Smithsonian Institution)

small patches of arable bottomland, but the extensive cornfields on the high mesas had been abandoned by 1500.

When the first white explorers reached this area in the eighteenth century, they found about 4,000 Ute, of the Ute-Aztecan language group. The Ute were late-comers to the region, and they had probably followed the Navaho south not more than 1,000 years ago. The Ute lived on about the same scale as the Shoshoni and Bannock of the upper Snake country. They hunted a great deal in the mountains to the east and gathered some berries, seeds, and nuts. They grew some corn and vegetables in garden plots along the streams.

The Ute lived in small villages, each dwelling a framework of timber with mat coverings. Because of their gardens, they were secure against starvation, but their food supply was never more than barely adequate.

During this early period the Ute had few enemies. They had some dealings with the Navaho to the south, but there is no tradition of warfare between the two tribes in early times. To both the east and the west, mountain barriers separated them from any attacking forces. It seems probable that they sometimes strayed north to the Great Salt Lake country, where they would meet small bands of Shoshoni and do a little trading.

The Ute were scattered in several small bands, each keeping to its own valley for the most part. Each band was large enough to have its own chief, but there was no attempt to unite the bands.

38

6 Horses for the Western Indians

THE COLORFUL mounted Indians of the Great Plains made a strong impression on the early travelers moving westward from the Mississippi Valley to the buffalo country. They found bands of nomadic horsemen wherever the buffalo ranged, from southern Texas northward to the Canadian forests.

To the west, beyond the Rockies and far beyond the last of the buffalo herds, horses were in common use among the Ute in western Colorado, the Shoshoni and Bannock of the upper Snake country, the Flatheads of western Montana, and all the tribes of the Columbia Basin. These tribes had a highly developed horse culture roughly equivalent to that of the tribes of the Asian steppes, where horses had been ridden for 4,000 years.

So it is not surprising that the explorers and trappers assumed the Western Indians had used horses for about the same length of time.

Skeletons of horses found in old gravel beds along the Snake River showed that horses had lived in that valley millions of years ago. Other fossil finds indicated that these horses had evolved in this region from much smaller animals and had reached Asia much later by a land bridge between Alaska and Siberia.

But further research revealed a strange development. All the horses in North America had suddenly died off about 15,000 years ago, along with camels and other species of large grass eaters. The extinction of these species is one of the fascinating puzzles of the prehistoric West, for other species of grass eaters of similar size, such as bison, elk, deer, and antelope, survived in large numbers.

Thus, all North America was entirely without horses of any kind for some 15,000 years until Spanish colonists brought their stock to the mainland early in the sixteenth century. In 1541 two Spanish exploring expeditions brought the first tame horses to the buffalo country. That year the remnants of Hernando de Soto's forces reached central Texas from the east, then turned back to the Mississippi River. At the same time Francisco Vásquez de Coronado led his men into the Texas Panhandle from the Rio Grande Valley of New Mexico. He turned north as far as central Kansas before turning back to his base among the pueblos.

A legend has grown up about possible strays from the horse herds of the two expeditions getting together in the Texas Panhandle and starting a herd of wild horses, which increased in numbers until the wild bands had spread over the Great Plains. Then the Indians were supposed to have captured some of the wild horses. In a short time they had learned how to tame and ride the animals, and in about a century they had developed a complex horse culture closely matching that of the Spanish. Thus, these primitive tribes are supposed to have accomplished in 100 years a task that had taken civilized man in the Near East more than 2,000 years. This legend has appealed greatly to a number of scholars who have little knowledge of horses and even less knowledge of the wild horses on the Texas plains. They choose to ignore Spanish customs and practices concerning horses for war and for such expeditions.

In the wide-open spaces of western Texas it would require something of a miracle to join up the stray horses in one band, especially strays from two expeditions which did not approach closer to each other than 350 miles. And from the moment a horse strayed from the camp, it would be in constant danger from wolves, cougars, Indian hunters, droughts, blizzards, bad water, and poisonous plants. Yet if several horses did stray, and did by a miracle join in one band, and did survive the many dangers, they could not produce a single colt, for all these trained war-horses were stallions. A strict rule banned mares from such an expedition.

41

Even large herds of wild horses on the plains would have been of no use to the Indians except for food. These primitive men had not the slightest idea of how to catch and tame a wild horse or any reason to do so. They had no horse gear of any kind. It is not surprising that a detailed survey of the Indian tribes of the Texas Panhandle about 1629 showed not a single horse, wild or tame, in the whole country, yet this was eighty-eight years after De Soto and Coronado and thirty years after all the Plains tribes are supposed to have acquired and tamed horses.

None of the Western tribes used any horses until they had been able to secure a few tame, gentle, well-trained animals, together with rather complete instructions for the care and use of the horse. The Indians also had to be taught how to make and use horse gear. The necessary gentle horses and the instructions for their care and use came from the Spanish colonists along the Rio Grande in the early seventeenth century.

In 1598 Juan de Oñate sent the first of his settlers into the Rio Grande Valley. In a few years he had built up the colony until it consisted of several small Spanish settlements scattered along the river, each one close to a Pueblo village. The Spanish raised some field crops, but they depended chiefly on their livestock. For both the crops and livestock they secured Indian workers from the nearby pueblos.

Large herds of range sheep and range cattle grazed on the hills for miles around to supply the settlements

42

Contemporary Yakima, wearing traditional costumes, ride their horses in a parade.

(Geoffrey Hilton)

with wool, sheepskins, rawhide, leather, meat, butter, and cheese. Until barbed wire was developed in the 1870's, it was physically impossible to fence the farmlands along the Rio Grande, for the nearest timber suitable for fences was high in the mountains many miles to the north. Hence, each band of sheep and each herd of cattle had to be herded for twenty-four hours a day, seven days a week during the crop season. If they once reached the fields, they could destroy the entire crop in a few hours.

Bands of sheep could best be herded by men on foot, with clever dogs to help, but range cattle could be handled only by mounted men. These Spanish cattle were lean, swift, and mean, a real danger to any man on foot. If they did not choose to run him down and kill him, they could easily run miles away. It took many well-mounted vaqueros to handle the herds.

Although the Spanish rancher did not actually live in the saddle, he of necessity spent a large part of each day riding, taking care of the many daily chores and recurring tasks. Cattle had to be rounded up and driven to new ranges away from the crops. A packload of supplies had to go to the sheep camp out on the range. Any errands, trips to town, visits to the neighbors, or hunting trips were done on horseback. And finally, the large herds of range horses had to be controlled.

All the saddle horses had to live on natural pasture, because grain was too scarce to feed any animals except for extra work under unusual conditions, such as a long, fast trip. A horse ridden hard at rangework needed two or three days to recover its strength and to eat enough grass to replenish its tissues. Thus, one cowhand would use a saddle string of five to ten horses for his ordinary work, riding each one about twice a week.

To raise enough horses for the riders, the rancher had to raise a large number of mares, too, to keep the breeding herd up to strength. Each ranch then had a large herd of broodmares on the range the year around, and with the mares were the colts of that season, plus yearlings, two-year-olds, and three-year-olds, for the Spanish, like other Western stockmen, believed that horses raised on the open range matured rather slowly and should not be broken until they were at least four years old. Usually the spare saddle horses and the packhorses were kept in a separate herd, so on a large ranch there might be several herds on the range at a time.

Raising, breaking, handling, and using horses kept the ranchers busy most of the time, and they needed several helpers on each ranch. Daily chores in caring for all the horses were burdensome. Indians were used for such tasks whenever possible, but according to Spanish law, Indians were strictly forbidden to ride. It was a far cry from the seat of government in Mexico to the remote ranches along the Rio Grande, and with no government official near, ranchers often ignored the law, using Indians to bring in the saddle horses from the range, to take them to water, and the like. Also, when the rancher went on a long trip, he needed helpers to take care of the spare horses and the camp chores and perhaps to ward off attacks by wild Indians along the way. Frequently he did not have enough Spanish helpers for all these, and he took an Indian or two instead. Some of the Indians, working as stableboys, learned to ride a little on the sly. Thus, several of the Indians on each ranch became skilled horsemen.

These Indian helpers, even from the peaceful, sedentary Pueblo people, resented their serfdom, but if they ran away from their Spanish master, they had to seek refuge among the wild tribes, for the Spanish controlled all the Pueblo villages. Such a runaway had many miles of open country to cross before he could feel safe from pursuit by the mounted rancher. The Indian's only hope of escape was to ride away in the night on one of the best horses, driving several more as spares. Then dawn should find him far beyond reach of any pursuit.

Once he had reached a wild tribe, the nomadic Indians beyond Spanish control, the fugitive ran the risk of being killed, but often he was well received. He could use his well-broken horses and his knowledge of horsemanship to ensure a position of respect among his new companions. In a few weeks he could teach some of the braver young men to ride and could show them how to steal and use range horses. Thus, in about five years this wild band would be mounted rovers of the grasslands.

This process of distributing horses to the wild tribes started soon after the Spanish came to the Rio Grande Valley. By 1659 the local Spanish officials were reporting border raids by mounted Navaho from the northwest in the Four Corners area (where the borders of Utah, Colorado, New Mexico, and Arizona meet today). These Navaho in turn passed some of their horses along in trade to their immediate neighbors to the north, the Ute, who in turn traded horses to the Shoshoni and Bannock. In this way horses had reached the Indians in southwestern Montana about 1690.

The upper Snake Valley and the upper Missouri drainage in southwestern Montana were good stock country, suitable for raising horses on the open range. Under

46

favorable conditions the Shoshoni herds multiplied rapidly, and neighbors to the east, north, and west became interested in securing horses of their own. The Flatheads to the northwest borrowed some Shoshoni horses by 1710; the Blackfeet to the northeast did likewise by 1730. The Crows on the Yellowstone River to the east probably secured their first horses from the Shoshoni by trade.

Some of the Shoshoni horses moved west from the upper Snake Valley around Idaho Falls to the Boise and Payette valleys 300 miles away. Nez Perce from the Clearwater country went south up the Little Salmon and across to the headwaters of the Weiser and Payette rivers, where they sometimes met the Shoshoni to trade. They managed to get a few horses to start their own herds about 1720. The Cayuse tribe in northern Oregon had horses a little later, either from their Nez Perce friends or from the Shoshoni across the Blue Mountains to the east. By 1800 all the tribes in the Columbia Basin had some horses, and many of the people had adjusted their ways to make good use of the new servants.

According to Flathead tradition, they stole their first horse. A Flathead scouting party found a large Shoshoni camp and watched it for several days. They learned a great deal about the horses in this way and finally decided to steal one gentle old mare to take home. For the first few days they were careful to stay at a safe distance from this new animal. They marched along in a circle, with the mare in the middle. After they became better

47

acquainted with the mare, they became bolder and put a rope around her neck to lead her the rest of the way.

The Nez Perce say they traded for a gentle, pregnant mare from the Shoshoni near Boise to start their herd. For months, crowds of people watched the mare every waking moment until after the colt was born the next spring. In this way many of them soon learned how to manage a gentle horse.

Indians at The Dalles bought their first horse only for show. It was carefully tended and guarded and led proudly in the procession on a feast day to impress the visitors.

The Sanpoil, not very daring, learned to ride on a slow, gentle horse. One person led the horse while the rider held a long stick in each hand to steady himself by pressing each stick in turn against the ground.

These stories, all of tame horses, emphasize how difficult it would have been for any Texas Indians to learn on their own how to capture and train wild horses in just a year or two.

7 Horses Bring Many Changes

IN THE UTE country the valleys and foothills furnished good pasture for horses, while the Rocky Mountain mass protected fairly well against the blizzards of the plains. Thus, with very little work the Ute raised a good crop of colts each year. In addition, they continued to secure a few more horses from the Navaho by trade and also staged a few raids on the Spanish ranches around Taos. Once the Ute had plenty of horses and had learned to use them, they became seminomadic, opening trails across the Rockies to the buffalo herds on the Great Plains in eastern Colorado.

This bold advance brought them large supplies of meat and robes, but it put them in constant danger of attack from the Plains tribes, who claimed the hunting grounds as far west as the front range of the Rockies. These tribes were larger and more powerful than the Ute and prevented the intruders from establishing a permanent hold east of the mountains, but the many packs of dried buffalo meat each year supplemented their own local meat supply and raised their standard of living. The Ute still raised corn, beans, and squash in their garden patches and had some fruit trees, mostly peach, in addition to wild berries. A trickle of trade goods such as knives, cooking pots, cloth, and a few guns reached them from the Spanish settlements to the south, usually through Navaho middlemen. After 1820 American traders working west from St. Louis came to the Ute nearly every year to trade.

The Paiute and Western Shoshoni bands in the Utah and Nevada desert, the Diggers, owned no horses and underwent almost no cultural changes on account of the introduction of this new animal. Any stray horse which fell into their hands was considered game and went into the cooking fires at once, supplying a large feast to a small band. These desert Indians had nothing to trade to their neighbors or to the American fur men. The few fur-bearing animals in their land, mostly beaver, were trapped by the white men. The first chance these Indians had to secure a supply of trade goods came after 1840, when the emigrant trains began to move along the Overland Trail to California. Along the dreary wastes many articles were abandoned by the weary travelers, cast aside along the trail or simply left in camp. Sometimes a wagon broke down, and the whole load was abandoned. The Indians then helped themselves to what they could use, usually clothing, bedding, cooking utensils, and some pieces of iron.

In southern Idaho and all through the Columbia Basin, where horses could be raised on the open range, the new animals produced a cultural revolution so rapid and so extensive that it is difficult to decide exactly what items of the old cultures the tribes altered, what they abandoned, and what they kept unchanged. The greatest change in any tribe, and the most rapid, was among the Nez Perce. Here a combination of very good horse country and intelligent, adaptable people soon developed this tribe into stockmen who operated on a large scale. This in turn led to many additional related changes.

The Nez Perce country has deep, sheltered valleys with ample forage and water for the winter range and high, well-watered plateaus covered with luxuriant grass for the summers. The whole country was protected from enemies to the north, east, south, and southwest by encircling mountain barriers. The only open approach, a broad corridor to the west, led to the lands of friendly tribes, the Palouse, Walla Walla, and Yakima. One mountain trail, long and rough, went up the Little Salmon River and on south to the Shoshoni in the Boise country. Two trails, each winding across 100 miles of timbered mountains, gave access to the Bitterroot Valley in Western Montana and to the buffalo country on to the east. The eastern end of one of these, the Lolo Trail,

51

led to the lower Bitterroot Valley near Hell Gate, while the other, the Nez Perce Trail, ended some 60 miles up the Bitterroot to the south. These three trails were difficult for enemy raiders and unsuitable for a rapid retreat with stolen horses. In addition, skilled Nez Perce hunters killed off the predators, the cougars and wolves, giving the horse herds protection from those enemies, too.

In such a suitable environment the Nez Perce horse herds multiplied rapidly. In a few years the tribe had more horses than could be used, even more than were wanted, but still the colts came each year. Thus each year it was necessary to dispose of 500 or 600 horses to the neighbors to keep the herds small enough for the pastures.

The older and poorer horses were traded off first, and their going left better-quality breeding stock on the ranges. The Nez Perce also gelded some of the poorer stallions and improved the stock in that way. The combination of good pastures and the systematic culling of the poorer stock enabled the Nez Perce to raise horses of good quality and adequate size, larger and stronger than the Indian ponies of the northern plains. Nez Perce horses averaged about 15 hands in height and weighed about 1,000 pounds when full grown, in contrast with the Blackfeet ponies, 14 hands or less in height and weighing from 600 to 1,000 pounds.

For the first several years, horses in the Columbia Basin were luxury items, owned to impress the neigh-

Michael Pablo of the Flathead tribe and buffalo herd. He raised them and sold them to the Canadian government in 1908. Photographed on the Joiko River in western Montana.
(Montana Historical Society, Helena)

bors, but this changed rapidly once the people learned to ride. The Nez Perce in particular found it easier to ride across the plateau to visit other villages than it was to paddle or pole a dugout canoe up the river. They also

53

rode to and from their hunting grounds, using spare horses to carry home the meat. Whole families rode to the camas grounds each summer, with packhorses carrying their mats, robes and tools to the meadows and the many loads of dried camas on the return trip.

As the families rode the horses more, they gathered in larger and fewer summer camps. In time the Weippe camas meadows attracted people from 100 miles or more away. This site furnished grass for all the hundreds of horses, plenty of wood for the camp and cooking fires, and good springwater.

For six weeks the camp would be filled with people from twenty to thirty villages and many visitors from other tribes. The young people had a larger group of their own age to visit with. Resulting marriages spread families over wider areas and prevented neighboring villages from becoming too inbred. The large villages of Kamiah, 65 miles up the Clearwater, and Asotin, on the Snake just above the forks, had many young people from each village marry someone from the other.

By 1800 the Nez Perce were even marrying into other tribes, the Cayuse, Walla Walla, Palouse, and Yakima, all of their own language group, but surprisingly, they also married into the Montana Salish, the Flatheads, who lived far across the mountains. The lasting friendship between the two tribes began when a few from each tribe met for trade at Spokane Falls.

Once the Nez Perce had become stockmen and travelers, trade became an important item with them.

They could offer horses or their fine laminated bows of mountain sheep horn. They also carried less valuable trade items such as ladles, dishes, and bowls of horn; cakes of camas, kouse, and huckleberries; tanned skins of mountain sheep and deer; and the famous flat twined wallets woven of Indian hemp and decorated with an overlay of bear grass, sometimes dyed with their vegetable dyes. In later years cornhusk replaced the bear grass, and the wallets were more commonly known as cornhusk bags.

At the big fishing center at Celilo Falls on the Columbia the Nez Perce traded their goods for bales of dried salmon, skins of salmon oil, decorative seashells, and necklaces of shell disks. At Spokane Falls they found articles of mountain goat horn, and some smoked buckskin, but what attracted them most were the heavy tanned buffalo robes brought down from the Flathead country far up Clark Fork. The Flatheads said the robes came from large animals which ranged the plains beyond the far mountains about 400 miles away. The Flatheads especially wanted shells and beads from the coast, but they soon learned to value the powerful Nez Perce bows, just the thing for killing buffalo from horseback.

Although the Nez Perce and the Flatheads were from entirely different language groups, they soon became good friends. The Flatheads invited parties of Nez Perce hunters to join them for a trip to the buffalo country, a wonderful experience for the Nez Perce, but the long

55

trail from their country to western Montana led for 100 miles through the lands of the rather unfriendly Coeur d'Alene.

Then the Nez Perce learned that their Flathead friends had a trail from Hell Gate across Lolo Pass to a fishing spot near the head of the Lochsa River, above the canyon. The Nez Perce at once set out to find a trail around the canyon of the Lochsa. They climbed up the timbered ridge east of the Weippe meadows and followed the backbone of a high timbered ridge between Lochsa and North Fork. This was known as the Lolo Trail, famous to this day. It bypassed the Coeur d'Alene country entirely and led the Nez Perce directly to the lower Bitterroot Valley.

This shorter, safer trail encouraged more of the Nez Perce to go to the buffalo country each year and speeded up the flow of goods from the Columbia Basin to the Great Plains. In time a few of the articles from the Pacific coast were traded on East, passing from tribe to tribe until they ended up in Massachusetts. From the Great Plains the Nez Perce brought back warbonnets of eagle feathers and finely tanned buffalo robes ornamented with dyed quillwork. They also traded for pipes of catlinite, tipis, and the rawhide carrying cases, the parfleches.

But hunting on the Montana plains soon proved dangerous. The whole area was infested with large war parties of hostile Blackfeet, armed with muskets brought to them by the Hudson's Bay Company traders. The

Blackfeet waged wars of extermination against both the Shoshoni and the Flatheads, intent on clearing them from all western Montana so the Blackfeet could move in. When the Flatheads and Shoshoni tried to stem the Blackfeet advance, they found that their horses were no match for the enemy's guns. After about seventy years of this unequal contest the Blackfeet had driven the Shoshoni frontier from the Bow River in Alberta south to southern Idaho and had chased the Flatheads back across Marias Pass.

The warlike Blackfeet were dangerous because of both their guns and the large number of fighting men they put in the field each summer. By 1775 the tribe contained about 25,000 people, three or four times the combined population of the Flatheads, Coeur d'Alene, Kutenai, Nez Perce, and Lemhi Shoshoni who tried to oppose them. Where the Western tribes at times might muster a war party of 300 men, the Blackfeet each year sent out three or four at a time as large as that.

Soon the Blackfeet power and aggression had blocked the Western hunters from all the land east of the mountains and north of the Sun River. The Flatheads and Nez Perce then crossed the mountains farther south, from the head of Clark Fork to the Big Hole River, then moving east into the Madison and Gallatin valleys, and on across Bozeman Pass to the upper Yellowstone.

On the Yellowstone they met the Crows, who were usually friendly and interested in trade. They astonished the Western Indians with trade goods from the Mandan

57

villages in Dakota, where white traders had been coming since 1729. Of special interest to the Nez Perce were the Crow guns, muzzle-loading flintlock muskets.

Here the Nez Perce showed a good example of their superior initiative and resourcefulness. They decided on positive measures to get some guns, while the others just talked about the new weapons. In the summer of 1805 the Nez Perce sent three young men, loaded with Western trade goods, to the Crow country. They were to go with the Crows to the Mandan villages and buy what guns they could. In August the three returned with six guns, the first on record owned by any Columbia Basin tribe.

The young men reported that a group of strange people from the East had stayed at the Mandan villages the previous winter and that the party was now on its way to the Nez Perce country, expecting to cross the mountains by September. These were the explorers, Meriwether Lewis and William Clark, and their men, who came to the Weippe meadows and visited the Nez Perce. Then they moved down to the mouth of North Fork and constructed dugout canoes for the voyage on down to the ocean. They left their horses in charge of a local chief.

When Lewis and Clark returned in the spring of 1806, they spent about six weeks at Kamiah waiting for the heavy snows to melt from the Lolo Trail. During this period the Indians and whites became good friends. The Nez Perce supplied the whites with quantities of food

Reminiscent of the Oregon country when the West was young are these Indian tipis on the Kah-nee-ta resort which may be rented by overnight guests today. Of authentic Indian design, there is an inner wall and adjustable smoke flags, which when properly adjusted, provide air conditioning of a sort.

(Photo by Edmund Y. Lee, Portland)

and brought in all the horses left in their care months before. For these and other services, the explorers gave the Nez Perce three guns and a supply of ammunition. They also gave simple medical treatments to several of the Indians, in some cases with remarkable results.

The Nez Perce continued trading with the Crows for warbonnets, parfleches and buffalo robes, but in four years they could buy guns nearer home. Canadian fur traders built a post, Spokane House, below the falls at the mouth of the Little Spokane River in the fall of 1809. Then men sent out by John Jacob Astor of New York opened opposition posts, one just across from Spokane House, the other at the mouth of the Okanogan. Meanwhile, the Canadians put in posts for the Flatheads and the Kutenai.

Many of the Indians trapped fur-bearing animals to trade at the new posts, but the Nez Perce considered such work beneath them. They had plenty of horses to trade for what they wanted. If the white men wanted to trade for horses, fine. If not, the Nez Perce just traded horses to the Indians who did get trade goods from the post. Since the fur traders used from 300 to 400 horses a year in their work, the Nez Perce could get all the guns and other supplies they wanted without doing any trapping.

Once the Western tribes were well supplied with guns, they were able to meet the Blackfeet on more equal terms. They organized large hunting parties to invade the Montana plains. In the span of twenty years or so,

60

all the Columbia Basin tribes had acquired some of the skin-covered tipis, although many families still used the mat-covered lodges, especially for the rainy season, for the skin coverings would rot in heavy rains or wet snows.

The Weippe meadows was the usual gathering place for the large parties going East, although some of the hunters from the main Columbia gathered at Spokane House and went up Clark Fork from there. Such hunting parties might have people from twenty separate villages and five tribes. A whole family group might choose to go, or half a family, or even just two or three young men, while the rest of the village stayed home. Seldom did the small children or the old people go across the mountains.

After a year in Montana many of the hunters would return home, but many more would stay on for another year or two, and new hunters would come east to join them. This seminomadic life broke up many of the old village patterns and developed new social groups, each under an elected leader. Changes came in property rights, too. No longer did each family live in its portion of the large community building. Now each owned its own lodge, its own band of horses, its own meat and robes. Only the village site and the fishing grounds were left as community property.

Some of this cultural change spread through all the Columbia Basin tribes as men from the Palouse, Walla Walla, Cayuse, Umatilla, Yakima, and Mid-Columbian tribes joined in the hunting parties. For a period of about

61

sixty years, from 1815 until the Nez Perce War in 1877, this pattern of hunting continued, although new settlements along the way and the slaughter of the buffalo herds hampered the hunting bands by 1870.

In 1837 a severe epidemic of smallpox killed off a half or more of the Blackfeet and reduced that tribe to a point where it could no longer send out the great war parties each year. The bitter fighting slackened then, for the Western tribes made no attempt to attack the Blackfeet on their own lands. The Flatheads and Nez Perce were able to hunt along the Sun River and east into Judith Basin, both superior buffalo ranges. Blackfeet hostility toward the Western tribes and toward any traders who might sell them guns kept northern Montana in a turmoil until a reasonably firm peace was secured by an intertribal treaty in 1855.

Although the war between the Western tribes and the Blackfeet dominated the period to 1837, the Nez Perce also had hostile bands to fight on their southern border. While they were usually on friendly terms with the Lemhi Shoshoni of southeastern Idaho, often joining them in fights against the Blackfeet, the Nez Perce had trouble with the Shoshoni in the Boise area.

The two tribes were at peace for a time about 1720, when the Nez Perce went south to trade and bought their first horse, but by 1800 the two tribes were engaged in bitter fighting. In 1803 a Shoshoni war party marched on foot to Kamiah during the summer while the village was at the Weippe meadows digging camas. The raiders found one Nez Perce family camped by the river fishing and killed them all. A young hunter on the northern slope saw the attack and escaped to Weippe to arouse the camp.

A large band of mounted warriors dashed down the trail in a wild chase, but by the time they had crossed the Clearwater and had reached the open prairie, the Shoshoni had disappeared. The raiders, fearful of being caught out on the prairie by the horsemen, took refuge in a large hole in the wall of Cottonwood Canyon. The Nez Perce fired the timber in the hole and burned them all to death. One Nez Perce from Almota exposed himself on the canyon rim and was wounded in the groin by a spent arrow; the scratch developed an infection, and he died in a few days.

As was their custom after a decisive victory, the Nez Perce sent a delegation with the calumet, the sacred peace pipe, to the Shoshoni to suggest a permanent peace between the two tribes, but some rash young Shoshoni ambushed and murdered the three envoys, a heinous crime in the eyes of all tribes who used the calumet.

A few weeks later the Nez Perce received their first six guns and used the new weapons to show the Shoshoni that it was both bad manners and expensive to break the sacred shield guarding calumet. (The calumet was considered a sacred shield protecting the bearer against all aggression.) The avengers collected forty-two Shoshoni scalps as down payment on the debt, and the Shoshoni never again dared raid north of the

63

Little Salmon, but the Nez Perce, during the next thirty years, often rode in strength to the Boise country only to find empty wickiups. The prudent Shoshoni took to the hills and hid out until the danger was over. Hudson's Bay Company traders from Fort Nez Perce finally arranged a truce, because this hostility interfered with the fur trade profits, but a vestige of this hostility remained for a long time and enabled the Army to hire Bannock scouts to fight against the Nez Perce in 1877.

8 Fur Traders in the Columbia Basin

F UR TRADERS in the Columbia Basin found all the tribes friendly and eager to buy their goods, especially guns. The Indians had seen a few guns when the Lewis and Clark Expedition came West. Then the purchase of six guns by the Nez Perce in 1805 further whetted their interest in the powerful weapons, more for hunting than for war. Intertribal warfare among the Columbia Basin tribes was infrequent and rather desultory, rather than a way of life as it was on the plains.

Of great value to the primitive people were other trade articles, especially woolen cloth and woolen blankets. Smoked buckskin clothing was fine in dry weather, even in zero cold, and tanned robes were a great comfort as long as they were kept dry. But buckskin soaked up rain like a sponge and stretched out of shape while it clung in clammy folds against the skin.

Once the Indian could get any cloth, he used it first for his breechclout, then for his leggings. Wool blankets were used both for wraps and for bedding. One great advantage of the wool was that it kept the wearer warm even when it was wet, and a good soaking did not ruin it. The garments of wool were more comfortable, too, because they did not get clammy from sweat. The new garments and bedding helped the Indians against chills, colds, and related illnesses.

Steel knives came high on the list of desirable goods. They were stronger and sharper than chipped stone and would last for years with proper care. Steel awls and steel needles for the women made their work easier and their finished garments neater. Metal pots and pans light enough to be carried on packhorses were a great help in cooking. With the use of metal pans the old practice of boiling food by putting heated stones in the container was no longer practiced except in an emergency.

Then there were the luxury items—ribbons, mirrors, paints, gaily colored beads, small brass bells, thimbles, and other small trinkets for personal adornment or for decorating the horse trappings. Trade tobacco at first supplemented, then supplanted the harsh native tobacco. Smoking became more common and was no longer reserved for important council meetings and ceremonies.

The many benefits brought in by the traders were partially offset by some harmful items, the worst being

This drawing of an Indian dance in the Columbia Basin is believed to have been made about 1855.

(Oregon Historical Society, Portland)

alcohol. The whites also brought in some diseases new to the area. And in time they produced quite a number of half-white, half-Indian children who were misfits in both the Indian villages and the trading posts. With no firm social standing, no feeling of belonging to a social group, these half-breeds frequently became trouble-makers wherever they went.

67

Inevitably there were some clashes between the Indians and whites, but in the Columbia Basin these were rather minor incidents and usually soon forgotten. However, two of the clashes had some important results. The first of these occurred in the village at the mouth of the Palouse River. One of Astor's men, John Clarke, was sent from Astoria to establish a post near Spokane Falls which would compete with Spokane House, the North West Company post. Clarke took his men and supplies by boat up the Columbia and Snake to the Palouse village, where he left his boats in charge of the headman. He traded for packhorses to carry his goods across to the Spokane River.

When Clarke returned in the spring of 1813 with a large supply of furs, he was pleased to find that his boats were in good shape and ready for the return trip. As a token of his appreciation Clarke allowed the headman to drink some of Clarke's own private wine from Clarke's own prized silver goblet. The next morning the goblet was missing. Clarke drew his men up in fighting array and demanded that the village surrender the missing goblet and the thief at once. The Indians indicated one of the young men as the guilty person. He immediately stepped forward and gave up the loot. Clarke, in return, had him hanged immediately on a tripod of tipi poles. In the eyes of the Indians, Clarke was guilty of murder, for the Indian had broken no Indian code in stealing from a stranger who was not a guest of the village.

Two years later a boatload of Northwesters was moving up the Columbia near Umatilla. It was the custom for such boats to stop to visit briefly with any group of Indians who came down to the riverbank, the traders furnishing free tobacco, of course. The boat had just started up a rapid when the Indians hailed it. The boatmen wanted to reach the head of the rapid before stopping. The Indians thought the whites were trying to pass without providing the customary smoke and clutched at the side of the boat. The crew thought the Indians were attacking them, so they shot and killed three of the Indians. Here, again, the Indians considered that the men had been murdered.

When Donald Mackenzie of the North West Company came up the Columbia two years later, in the summer of 1817, to build Fort Nez Perce at the mouth of the Walla Walla River, he was met by a hostile war band of some 2,000 Indians assembled from several of the neighboring tribes, ready to wipe out Mackenzie's party if he did not retreat. Mackenzie took up a strong position behind a barrier of driftwood on a sandspit in the river and held them off for several days without fighting. Finally, he convinced the Indians that it was to their advantage to have a trading post so handy to their villages.

Fort Nez Perce prospered for many years and in time came to be called Fort Walla Walla. When it was destroyed by fire in 1853, it was not rebuilt. The U.S. Army in 1856 began a post 30 miles up the Walla Walla, calling it Fort Walla Walla, and confusing some historians.

Another long-range effect of the two killings was to

turn the Nez Perce away from the Hudson's Bay Company men who succeeded the Northwesters in 1821. The tribe turned to the American traders who assembled yearly at a rendezvous in western Wyoming each summer. This in turn led the Nez Perce to send to St. Louis for teachers, with far-reaching results.

9 Fur Traders in Southern Idaho

F UR TRADERS from St. Louis followed closely on
the heels of the Lewis and Clark Expedition, up the
Missouri and the Yellowstone, anxious to exploit this
vast new land before the Canadian companies could
forestall them. Alexander Henry brought the first trade
goods to the Shoshoni country in 1810 by following up
the rivers, then crossing by the easy pass at Henry Lake.
He found the Indians poor, with little to offer in trade,
but their mountains were full of streams, and the streams
were full of beaver.

For the next thirty years the Americans came annu-
ally to trap in the streams. They had active competition
from the Canadians working east from Fort Nez Perce
from 1819 on. At times two rival groups of Americans

would be hindering each other while each worked independently against the Hudson's Bay men. A partial roster of the mountain men in the Shoshoni country during the height of the trapping reads like a roll of Western heroes—Kit Carson, Jim Bridger, Jedediah Smith, William Ashley, Joe Meek, Thomas Fitzpatrick, Robert Newell, Nathaniel Wyeth, Captain Benjamin Bonneville, and many more almost as important.

Alexander Henry built the first post in the area on Henry Fork of the Snake in 1810, but abandoned it after a year. One of Astor's men working out of Astoria built a small post at the mouth of the Boise River in 1812. It was wiped out in a few months by the Shoshoni. In 1819 Donald Mackenzie came by boat up the Snake through Hell's Canyon and built a new post on the same spot. This was old Fort Boise, which lasted more than thirty years. Then in 1834 Nathaniel Wyeth built Fort Hall on the upper Snake, 300 miles up stream from Fort Boise. These posts were never very profitable, for the local Shoshoni and Bannock were poor trappers and had little besides a few furs to trade.

Donald Mackenzie proved as early as 1819 there was a more profitable way to manage the fur trade in the Snake country. He led a party of men to trap the beaver during the winter when the fur was prime, instead of depending on the mediocre ability of the local Indians. The Snake River expedition became a yearly activity, first of the North West Company and later of the Hudson's Bay Company.

American companies sent their own band of trappers in from Wyoming each year. Instead of an established post, they held a big meeting each summer in the mountains, the first of them on the upper Green River, hence the Green River rendezvous, although some years it was on the Wind River and one year at Pierre's Hole on the Snake drainage.

The supply train, at first made up of pack animals and later of covered wagons, arrived each year from St. Louis about July 1, to meet the trappers and buy their furs. In addition to the necessary supplies such as guns, ammunition, knives, clothes, and camp gear, the traders brought some luxury items, with alcohol at the head of the list. While the trappers' furs and the alcohol lasted, the rendezvous was a rather wild place.

With sharp competition among the opposing fur companies, the Shoshoni and Bannock had a favorable market for what little they had to sell, usually a few horses and some buffalo robes. Parties of Nez Perce and Flatheads coming south from their Montana hunting were much better customers and were more respected by the traders. When a mountain man wanted an Indian wife, he usually chose one of the Nez Perce or Flathead girls. After the fur trade declined, these men usually moved on west to the new farming settlements in Oregon with their Indian wives and their children.

The presence of large parties of mountain men gave the Shoshoni and Bannock some protection against the Blackfeet, whose raids sometimes carried them as far south as Fort Hall and west to the Craters of the Moon. Blackfoot, Idaho, a few miles from Fort Hall, is a reminder of the Blackfeet aggression. After the smallpox stopped the Blackfeet in 1837, the Shoshoni and Bannock moved back to their former hunting grounds in southwestern Montana, only to be displaced in twenty years by the gold rushes of the 1860's and forced back into Idaho.

The mountain men also trapped south into the Ute country and sometimes moved farther south to Taos for the winter. The rather scant supply of furs in the Ute country and the total absence of buffalo made this unattractive to the fur men. The Ute were able to keep apart from the overland travel to California, too. None of the great Western trails crossed their lands. Thus, by the accident of geography this tribe was able to avoid conflict with the westward-moving whites until settlers came to Utah.

10 Religion of the Columbia Basin Tribes

AMONG ALL the Columbia Basin tribes there was a large body of common beliefs concerning the Creator and his helpers. They called the Creator Old One, which writers often translate as Great Spirit.

In the beginning Old One created the whole world and supplied it with plants and animals. Some evil spirits abroad in the world sometimes interfered with the orderly development of Old One's plans, so Old One had his helper, Coyote, go about making some adjustments and thwarting the evil spirits. In several stories about Coyote, he is described as a cultural folk hero with magic powers who does many things for the people, such as bringing the salmon up the Columbia by breaking the barrier set across the river by the evil ones.

Then, on a different plane, Coyote is a sly trickster often caught in his own snares and needing to be rescued by one of the other animals such as Magpie.

In his most important role Coyote is depicted as the creator of the various Indian tribes, using the carcass of a monster for the materials, while in his trickster role he is blamed for not bringing buffalo to the Columbia Basin when he had the chance. In many of the stories Coyote finishes the account by saying, "Soon the people are coming and things will be thus and so."

Old One had a great many spiritual helpers, and when creation was finished, he assigned one of these helpers to protect each kind of animal. One of these, Grizzly Bear, is credited with bringing huckleberries to the Nez Perce country. Chipmunk, a brave, dashing fellow, rescued himself from a big flood caused by the evil ones. He climbed on a log and floated off to safety, using his tail as a sail and singing his special magic song for protection. This song of Chipmunk's has become traditional for the gamblers of the Spokane tribe to use in their stick games.

Altogether there were several hundred such folktales about animals to be used as bedtime stories for children. Each one usually contained one or more short songs to be sung by an important character at the appropriate time.

The Mid-Columbian Indians made an important addition to the usual religious practices of the area. When some natural catastrophe beyond their comprehension

76

Interior of Yakima longhouse with ceremony in progress.
(Photo by James S. Rayner)

occurred, they considered it a warning from Old One. About 1789 they were very badly frightened by a volcanic eruption in the Cascades which covered their villages with a thick layer of gray volcanic ash they called dry snow.

During their period of fright one of the men fell into a trance which lasted for several hours. When he awoke from his trance, he told the village he had been on a visit to Old One in the sky and had brought back instructions which would enable them to ward off possible disaster. His teachings included a new song and a dance. If his people would dance this new dance for long periods, singing the new song all the while, Old One would be pleased and would not send any more disasters.

After that, other men had trances, resulting in messages from Old One concerning earthquakes, meteor showers, and very brilliant northern lights. The messages always contained new songs and sometimes new dances. Here is a brief explanation of this belief as given by an Indian from Nespelem:

After the world was prepared for human occupation, Old One, the Chief, told the people, "I will send messages to earth by the souls of people that reach me, but whose time to die has not yet come. They will carry messages to you from time to time, and when their souls return to their bodies, they will revive and tell you their experiences. Coyote and myself will not be seen again until Earth-Woman is very old. Then we shall return to the earth, for it will require a new change by that time. Coyote will precede me by some little time, and when you see him, you will know that the time is at hand. When I return, all the spirits of the dead will accompany me, and after that, there will be no spirit land. All the people will live together. Then will Earth-Woman revert to her natural shape and will live as a mother among her children. Then things will be made right, and there will be much happiness."

The Earth-Woman is now very old, and even her

Exterior of the longhouse.
(Photo by James S. Rayner)

bones, the rocks, are crumbling away. Therefore, the time cannot be far away when the earth will be transformed again, and the spirits of the dead will come back. Old One has sent messages from time to time. The Indians have learned from these that to be good, to speak good, to pray, and to dance will hasten the return of Coyote. Therefore, the Indians in many places often danced, and when dancing, they prayed much.

According to this informant and others, the prophet who brought the messages following the "dry snow" was the first one they could identify by name. In the fifty years following his prophecies, many other men in this

79

area had trances. Each, on awakening, assembled the whole village for dancing and singing. The actual dancing was not very lively or complicated. Each person remained in one spot in the big circle, shuffling his feet and singing the new songs. If any of the dancers fainted away during the ordeal, he was expected to give some message from Old One to the people when he revived.

After each scare and the resulting protracted period of dancing, the people gradually calmed down. When no new terror came, the dancing was halted, and daily duties were resumed. Usually several years elapsed before another event set them off on a new round of prophecies and dancing.

Older than this prophet cult was the belief that each person should have his own *wy-ya-kin,* or personal spirit helper. The Indians believed that Old One looked after all men equally. He would not help one man against another, so it was useless to pray for his help in time of war and the like. However, Old One had a great number of spirit helpers, one for each kind of animal or bird. One had charge of all the elk; another had all the wolves; yet another, all the golden eagles; and so on. It was possible for an Indian youth, by proper purification, fasting, and prayer, to secure one of these for his personal spirit helper to aid him against all dangers and to help him in fights against other Indians.

At the start of his vigil, the youth had no idea which spirit might answer his call. When the spirit did appear, it assumed the shape of the animal under its care so the youth might recognize it at once. The worth of a spirit helper was soon known by how much help it gave in hunting and in war. The Nez Perce were especially happy with their spirit helpers, for the warriors of the tribe won many fights, and the hunters brought in a great deal of game.

When the white man came with his steel tools, guns, and the like, the Indians soon decided that the white man must have more powerful magic, or medicine, than the red man. The white man's "talking paper" was the greatest magic of all. One man could make marks on a piece of paper, or smooth piece of bark, or a white tanned skin and send it by an Indian messenger to another white man many miles and several days away. The paper would then "talk" to the second white man, telling him many things. Perhaps if the Indian also had the magic of the talking paper, he might be able to meet the white man on even terms. It might even be possible that with the white man's magic added to that of the Indian's spirit helper, the red man would be the more powerful.

11 Teachers for the Indians

AFTER THE Hudson's Bay Company absorbed the North West Company in 1821, Sir George Simpson was put in charge. In 1825 he made a tour of the fur posts in the Columbia Basin and noticed that the Indians showed some interest in education. So he decided to take one boy, a son of an important chief, from each tribe and put all of them in the company school at the Red River Settlement.

The Indians agreed to send the boys with Simpson on his return to the East in 1826, but the experiment was not very successful. The changes in food, living conditions, and climate, plus exposure to diseases of the white men, killed several of the boys. One of them, Spokane Garry, managed to survive and returned to his tribe about 1830 with his new skills and learning. He began to teach his people how to build log houses, to raise crops, especially potatoes, and to read and write. Garry had a Bible which he read to his people on Sundays.

The Nez Perce wanted their boys to have the white man's education, too, but they felt some antagonism toward the Hudson's Bay Company men. The hanging of the Palouse thief and the killing of the three Indians at the Columbia rapids had been the acts of Canadians. Also, the Nez Perce did not want to send their boys off to die of disease. They decided it would be quicker and safer to have a teacher come to the tribe. Then a large number of men and boys could learn at one time without the perils of the long trip and the settlements.

The Nez Perce knew that their good friend, William Clark, was in charge of Indian affairs, with his office at St. Louis. If they sent a request for teachers to him, he would surely help them. In the summer of 1831 four Nez Perce set out from Weippe on the long trail. In the buffalo country they stopped at a hunting camp where Nez Perce and Flatheads had banded together as protection against the Blackfeet. The Flatheads decided that three of their men should go to St. Louis with the Nez Perce. The seven men then went to the Green River rendezvous and joined the caravan carrying the furs to market. On the long eastward trek three of the men turned back, two died in St. Louis that fall, another died at Fort Union on the way home in 1832, and the seventh was killed by the Blackfeet in southwestern Montana in the fall. In St. Louis they found no one who could talk either Salish or Shahaptin, but they managed to communicate much of their request through sign language.

Seemingly the mission had ended in failure, but a somewhat garbled account of it reached a New York merchant, who added a few imaginative touches of his own, including a sketch of a coast Chinook, and published the whole story in a church paper. He presented the delegation as seeking religious instruction from the Christians. The accompanying sketch showed an Indian with a deformed head, and the merchant explained that the Nez Perce squeezed the heads of their babies into this shape.

Thousands of church people were stirred to action by this distorted appeal and began raising funds to convert these interesting heathens. The first man sent West met the Nez Perce at the rendezvous in 1834, but he decided to go on to the Willamette Valley and establish his mission in the white settlements and let the Nez Perce come to him if they cared to do so. Two more missionaries reached the rendezvous the next year and were deeply impressed by the welcome they received from the Nez Perce. They promised the tribe that people would come in 1836 to settle on the tribal lands and start a school.

Relying on this promise, a large band of Nez Perce rode out to South Pass in Wyoming to meet the traders' wagon train in 1836. On July 4 they met their new

Elizabeth Penney, a white girl, and two young Nez Perce friends playing with dolls, 1892.

teachers, two young married couples and a single man. The Nez Perce gave them free choice of any of the tribal lands for their use.

Henry and Eliza Spalding found a good spot in a large meadow on the Lapwai Creek, in the heart of the Nez Perce country. Marcus and Narcissa Whitman decided to put their mission among the Cayuse, although that tribe had not invited them. The Cayuse showed little interest in the whole project, but they allowed the Whitmans to use a portion of the Walla Walla Valley about 125 miles west of Lapwai and 30 miles east of the fur post, Fort Walla Walla, and on the Oregon Trail. Marcus

Whitman expected his station to give some help to travelers on their way to the Willamette Valley.

In the first burst of enthusiasm the Spalding mission made remarkable progress. While Spalding and the men hauled logs for a house and a schoolhouse, Mrs. Spalding started instruction to her first class. For this work she had to learn the Nez Perce tongue, invent spelling for all the words, and each day print by hand about twenty copies of a short lesson, the size of the class being limited to the number of important men who could crowd into the Spalding tipi. Then, when the class had finished its lesson, Mrs. Spalding turned to other duties, while each of her students in turn taught the lesson to a small group in his tipi. In this way about 250 Nez Perce learned to read and to write a little in their own tongue. Most of the instruction material was taken from the New Testament.

In addition to her schoolwork, Mrs. Spalding was keeping house in a tipi in November weather, with all her chores and household duties, and was preparing for the arrival of her baby in the spring. In addition, she had Nez Perce women visitors most of the time trying to learn a white woman's ways.

Once the first log house was ready, Mrs. Spalding had more time for teaching. She started a sewing class for girls, while Spalding was busy getting ready for the spring planting. He believed that the Indians should be taught to raise crops so they could become settled farmers with a more dependable food supply. Also, he needed farm products to help support the mission.

Spalding also carried on religious instruction for the whole village.

The Nez Perce readily accepted the basic teachings of the new religion, especially the part concerning human relations. They explained that they had always done the things asked for in the Commandments and had helped one another. Nor did they object to the concept of sin, although it was new to them, or to the Christian concept of life after death. But serious trouble arose when the teachers tried to impose the strict Puritan standards of conduct and the values of a small Eastern farming village. Also, the Nez Perce objected to Spalding's concept of landownership and of other property rights.

Spalding considered himself the religious leader and benefactor of the Nez Perce and, as such, expected both gratitude and obedience from the Indians. They were grateful, but they would not take orders from anyone, not even their own leaders. Spalding was quick-tempered, stubborn, and domineering, a rather poor type to manage a proud, independent people. Only the deep sympathy and understanding between Mrs. Spalding and the Nez Perce women kept the mission going without a serious outbreak.

Once Spalding had built his house and his fences at Lapwai, he believed he owned the mission lands. He wanted the fences to keep the Nez Perce and their horses out of his crops. The Lapwai band knew they still owned the land and expected to collect payments each year from the mission. They expected that the

87

benefits promised them by the missionaries would be material goods, while Spalding was using rather flowery Christian imagery in promising spiritual benefits. This breakdown in communications across the language and customs barriers is the direct cause of many of the conflicts between red men and white, although it is often ignored by writers in discussing the troubles.

Another violation of Indian custom came from the many tribal leaders from other villages who came to the new school and stayed on indefinitely. Spalding expected each of these to start a farm of his own near the mission and thus to develop a close-knit farming community centered on the mission church. The Lapwai people objected to this plan and said the outsiders should go home and farm their own land.

Many of the usual activities of the Nez Perce, such as feasting, dancing, horse racing, and buffalo hunting, appeared sinful to Spalding, and he tried to put a stop to them. He was shocked when the Indians went about in hot weather with their arms and legs bare. Some of the Nez Perce resented Spalding's objections to their conduct and attacked the mission property with acts of vandalism, such as wrecking the fences or breaking the ditch which brought water to the mill. Dancing naked in the schoolyard was another form of protest, shocking only the mission workers.

In all these actions the Nez Perce broke no laws, for they had none to break. In their little villages they lived under social control enforced by public opinion.

88

If any visitor behaved in an unseemly way, the local leaders could do no more than frown on his actions or, in extreme cases, suggest that he go home.

In order to give the missionaries and other white men more protection, the Indian subagent to Oregon attempted in 1842 to set up a simple form of government. Under some pressure from the agent and Spalding, the Nez Perce elected twelve of their leaders to serve as tribal chiefs and to act as the tribal council. One of their number was then chosen as head chief. These men, acting as a group, were to have authority over the whole tribe. This was an extension of the pattern of electing one man as the leader, or chief, of the band going to Montana to hunt buffalo.

Then the agent, Dr. Elijah White, proposed a set of ten simple laws. Any violation of the laws was to be punished by the council of chiefs, either by confiscating some property of the culprit or by whipping him. The only other punishments possible at the time were banishment or execution, and the Nex Perce objected to both. The tribe had no jail and did not want one. These ten laws were designed mostly to protect white men from Indian hostility. Little attention was given to any protection of the Indian from the whites. The Nez Perce, on their own initiative, added an eleventh law to protect stock from dogs.

Meanwhile, the success of the Spalding and Whitman missions and the resulting publicity among the churches in the East had brought in a number of other missionaries, some Protestant, some Roman Catholic. Usually a new Catholic mission was put as close as possible to an established Protestant mission, rather than in a new area. Friction between the missions soon developed into quarrels. The Indians became confused by the conflicting claims, and many of them decided to stay clear of all missions until the white men could agree on what were the right Christian teachings. The rift between Catholic, Protestant, and "heathen" Indians remains to this day.

12 Indian Troubles in the Desert of Idaho

THE CASUAL attitude of the Shoshoni toward early white travelers in their country can be illustrated by several examples, beginning with the Lewis and Clark Expedition.

Sacajawea, a member of the Lemhi Shoshoni band was captured near Three Forks, Montana, by a Hidatsa war party when she was about thirteen. She was taken to Dakota as a prisoner and later was won in a gambling game by Toussaint Charbonneau, a French Canadian, who hired out that same year, 1804, to guide Lewis and Clark to the West. When the party left the Mandan villages in the spring of 1805, Charbonneau took his Shoshoni wife and small baby along. The presence of Sacajawea with the party helped ensure a friendly welcome among her people. Her older brother was chief of the band and helped the white men buy horses for their mountain crossing.

In 1811 Wilson Price Hunt led a party of fur men into southeastern Idaho on his way from St. Louis to Astoria. As soon as his party could find large trees near the Snake River, they made dugout canoes for their journey, leaving their horses in the care of the local Shoshoni. The Indians took such good care of the horses the whites never saw them again.

After a rather pleasant ride down the Snake for 250 miles, Hunt and his men came to the Snake River Canyon, near the present town of Twin Falls, with its boiling rapids and three high falls. They were forced to abandon their boats and to cache all their extra goods. Later the Shoshoni, with some help from a French Canadian left among them, found the cache and helped themselves to the contents. The Shoshoni were prompted by no hostile feeling in these instances. They merely accepted gratefully the gifts brought to their country by the white men.

This casual attitude toward fur men traveling through did not apply to the same men if they tried to settle on Indian land. In 1812 John Reed was sent with a small party to build a post at the mouth of the Boise River. No sooner had Reed's men finished the post and started trapping than the Shoshoni staged a surprise attack, killing Reed, Pierre Dorian, and five French Canadian helpers. Marie Dorian, Pierre's Indian wife, escaped with her two boys, one horse, and some dried fish. She found a shelter for the winter in the heavy timber on the Blue Mountains 100 miles or so to the northwest. There she killed the horse for food, put up a small shelter under a large tree, and emerged safely the next spring with the two boys.

A whole bag of new troubles came to the Indians with the opening of the Oregon Trail to wagon trains filled with settlers. Although the missionaries among the Nez Perce and Cayuse had to work long and hard to convert a small portion of those Indians to Christianity, they were able, with little effort, to convince thousands of Easterners that the Oregon country was a good place to live. Partly to ensure continued financial support from the Eastern churches, the missionaries in their reports extolled the climate and fine soil of the new country. Crops grew well, flocks and herds prospered on the open range with little care, and broad lands lay ready for the plow. The mission letters, published in many church papers throughout the East, induced hundreds of families to move to the Oregon country. If missionary women could stand the trip, farm women with their children could follow. Then came added good news. In 1840 wagons had been taken to the Columbia.

By 1843 the movement was well under way. The caravans of covered wagons followed the trail first recorded by Robert Stuart when he went East with messages from Astoria in 1812. Since then the trail had been used a good deal by the fur men as far as Fort Hall on the upper Snake. The great trail wound for

2,000 miles across plains, mountains, and deserts from Independence, Missouri, to The Dalles on the Columbia at the head of the great gorge.

The wagon trains brought problems and troubles to the Shoshoni, for the white invaders considered the Indians along the way as just another form of wildlife, with no human rights whatever. The whites pastured off the grass with their herds, killed all the game in sight, and often took potshots at any Indian they saw lurking around.

And of course, the Indians lurked around. They had to know what the invaders were doing so the Indian families could run and hide when danger threatened. If the Indian scouts were to escape being shot, they had to keep out of sight. The scouts also stole horses and cattle from the herds, as was the custom in their country. Once in a while they might kill a lone straggler, or even wipe out an entire family whose wagon dropped far behind. In all this the Indians thought they were rightfully defending their homeland against unfriendly intruders.

All the while the Shoshoni feared that some of the travelers would try to settle on Shoshoni lands. In 1852 they were sure such an attempt was being made when the Ward party of fifteen people, in two wagons, stayed in their camp along the Boise River for a few days after the rest of the train had gone on. These people really had no intention of settling until they reached the Willamette Valley, but the Shoshoni had no way of

An Idaho Indian family outside its mat hut. Photographer and date unknown.

(Oregon Historical Society, Portland)

knowing this. The travelers were just resting their teams after a rough desert crossing and believed the local Indians to be harmless. Then came a surprise attack, killing thirteen and wounding the other two, who managed to escape and report the disaster to Fort Boise 30 miles downstream.

Any new farming settlement could be subjected to sporadic surprise attacks and could not hope to survive unless it grew large enough to drive out the local Indians. Even a few warriors, with some determination, could in time wreck a small settlement with little danger to themselves. They could really direct their attacks against the crops and herds.

The little Mormon settlement of Fort Lemhi found this out the hard way. They established the post in 1855, with a small fort and stockade as protection against direct attack by any band of hostiles. The local Indians were the weak, peaceful Lemhi Shoshoni, Saca-jawea's people, who had always been friendly toward the whites. The Mormons started in to teach the Indians farming and to convert them to the Mormon belief.

Then the whole Mormon organization became involved in a quarrel with the federal government. Stray mountain men, who did not like the Mormon settlements in mountain country, convinced some of the Lemhi Shoshoni and a few Bannock that the Mormons would soon take over all the Indian country unless they were driven out at once. The Indians began their attack by stealing horses and cattle and damaging the crops. After a few people on each side had been killed and wounded, the Mormons abandoned their colony and returned to Utah.

By the 1860's attacks on wagon trains became more common. Two examples of harassment of such trains occurred in 1862 at Massacre Rocks, just west of American Falls. There a band of about 200 warriors trapped a small train in the narrow passage through the cliffs, capturing the whole group and killing one man and wounding one woman in the process. Then they looted the wagons of clothing and left, driving off all the stock, but they did not harm any more of the people.

A few miles west of Massacre Rocks, at Rock Spring, another train lost twelve men in a similar attack but managed to drive off the Indians and save their stock. The severity of this attack resulted from the failure of the Indians to secure the stock.

Although most of the Indians along the Idaho stretch of the Oregon Trail showed no great animosity against the travelers, many of the travelers seemed to hate and fear all Indians, even friendly ones, and looked on them as dangerous wild animals to be exterminated, rather than as fellow human beings. Some of the whites believed they had the right, even the duty, to kill any red man they found, friendly or hostile. One woman with a wagon train in the Blue Mountains wrote about a very strong young man with her party who had a light case of scarlet fever. She and the others encouraged him to wrestle with any Indians who came to camp with fish and game to trade. When he had a good grip on his opponent, the sick man was to breathe heavily in the Indian's face, giving him the disease to take back to his village.

A Boise newspaper editor displayed the same attitude. When the Paiute were causing trouble in northern Nevada in the 1860's, he published a request for several hundred blankets infested with smallpox and promised he would supervise the delivery of the blankets where they would be most effective in destroying the Indians.

In each case the writer expected public approval of his action, and there is no indication that either was criticized by his neighbors for such sentiments. It is evident that even a friendly Indian had a difficult time just to survive after the whites moved in.

13 Indian and Mormon Relations

EVEN WHEN the settlers were friendly and treated the Indians like human beings, with human rights, strong cultural differences produced friction and led to trouble. This is shown by the trend of events among the Mormon settlements. The Mormons moved to Utah in 1847, settling in the small mountain valleys on the east side of the Great Salt Lake. As their numbers increased with new migrations, they spread south, putting pressure on the friendly Ute, and north into the land of the Shoshoni and Bannock.

In both areas the Mormons treated the Indians well, giving them food and clothing, and tried to make farmers of them. They explained the advantages of houses over tipis and wickiups, and the more dependable food supply provided by farm crops compared to wild seeds and berries. The Ute chiefs responded by professing friendship and offered no immediate objections to the new farms. But some of the Ute could not resist the easy supply of fresh meat represented by the farmers' herds and helped themselves to animals now and then. If a settler happened to see a Ute making such a raid, he might start shooting, and someone could get hurt.

Although the Sioux of the plains had tribal councils to make rules of conduct for the tribe, and a body of young men, the Dog Soldiers, to act as police, the Ute had no such organization. Even if the chief and most of the tribe expressed disapproval of the stock theft, they had no way to punish the guilty men.

In 1849 the number of incidents in Utah Valley increased to the point where the Mormons decided to take drastic action. Raising an armed force for the purpose of driving all the Ute from the valley, they killed twenty-seven Indians and drove off the rest in a short time.

Discoveries of gold in central Idaho and northeastern Oregon from 1860 to 1862 increased white travel on the Oregon Trail. As a result, the Shoshoni stepped up their raids on wagon trains all the way from the Wyoming line to Boise and were especially active along the Bear River. When the Mormons pushed up the Bear Valley, the Shoshoni resented the new settlers. Their particular grievance was the little settlement of Franklin just north of the Idaho border. Emboldened by their success against the wagon trains, the Shoshoni sometimes paraded in war regalia in the Franklin streets, threatening to wipe out the settlement someday.

Attacks on travelers and the overland mail became so frequent that Colonel Patrick Connor was sent to Salt Lake City with a force of California volunteers. Late in January he marched his men into a northern blizzard which hid the advancing column from Indian scouts and surprised the Shoshoni camp on the right bank of the Bear River a few miles above Franklin. The Indians fought well from the ravines and thickets, but the force of about 250 soldiers finally crushed them. Connor lost 23 killed, 44 wounded, and had 79 men treated for frozen toes and feet. Losses to the Shoshoni were estimated all the way from 224 by Connor to about 400 by one of the corporals. A Mormon who counted the Indian dead the next day reported nearly 400 bodies, two-thirds of them women and children. This terrible punishment kept the whole trail from Wyoming to Oregon almost free from attacks thereafter.

In March, 1864, the mining camp at Idaho City decided that the Indians to the south were a nuisance. A band of volunteers was recruited and sent out to sweep the whole of southwestern Idaho and southeastern Oregon. The men marched around the country, fought two skirmishes, and managed to murder two women they found in an Owyhee canyon.

After these organized attacks, many Shoshoni moved east and joined Chief Washakie and his Eastern Shoshoni in the Wind River area of central Wyoming.

The Paiute southwest of the Boise country continued to harass travelers along the stage and freight road from northern California to the mining camps until 1878. It was their activities along this area which aroused the Boise editor who asked for the smallpox-infected blankets. He aimed his accusations against Chief Winnemucca and his warriors.

Throughout this period of bloody disorder many people were killed, with each side believing it was fighting for right and justice. The Indians were trying as best they could to protect their homelands against uninvited strangers. The whites believed they had a duty to settle the open spaces of the West and the right to exterminate any Indians who stood in their way.

14 Indian Troubles in the Nevada Desert

THE WESTERN Shoshoni, Paiute, and Paviotso
Indians of Nevada and southeastern Oregon, the "Digger" people, had no problem with white settlers until the
silver mines opened in western Nevada after 1860. Even
trappers were infrequent visitors during the great days
of the fur trade. After the Oregon Trail was opened up
for wagons in 1840, travelers for California soon made
a road south from the Snake, up the Raft River, and on
down the Humboldt. The California travel started
slowly, but it swelled into a vast torrent in 1849, when
the big gold strikes were announced.

These large wagon trains swarming across the Nevada
desert were not much of a problem to the local Indians.
They had no settled villages but roamed from place to

place most of the year. In the hot, dry summers they stayed out of the Humboldt Valley and away from the lines of wagons. Also, they caught few diseases from the travelers, for they were too shy to visit the camps. Even if an Indian did catch a disease, it would be confined to his own small group of ten or fifteen people.

The desert Indians showed no obvious hostility toward the whites. They seemed to consider the invaders rather strange people, but they never tried to gather their forces to attack even a small wagon train. Their chief aim in life was to obtain more food, and these wagon trains greatly increased the available meat supply. One horse or one cow from the herd would make a fine feast for the whole band. While some parts of the animal were eaten raw to cut the keen edge of the appetites, the rest was roasted in large chunks, and the entire band ate as long as they could swallow, then lay in a stupor for hours recovering from their excessive eating.

These Indians soon learned that it was better to steal a horse than a cow, for the horse could be driven farther and faster, so the thief would be hidden far away by daylight. If the herd were too closely guarded for such a theft, an arrow or two into an animal would so disable it that it would be butchered in the morning before the wagons moved on. The whites would take the meat, of course, but a pile of offal would remain, an ample supply of good food for the day.

The Digger Indians had little interest in killing people just for the sake of killing. Usually they preferred to run

104

Ouray and his wife, Chipeta, of the Uncompahgre Ute tribe. Photographer unknown. It is thought to have been made in Washington, D.C., around 1880.

and hide. Many a solitary straggler walked for days along the Humboldt Valley unmolested, but a stray wagon with its delicious team would be subject to a sneak attack.

The real danger along the trail in Nevada came from the warlike Ute, who would ride over from Green River to raid the horse herds. They did not care much for the oxen or cattle. Here again the whole object of the raid was to escape unharmed with the loot, so the Ute usually avoided open fighting. At Battle Mountain a Ute war party ran off with all the stock from one train and drove the animals to a secure place in a hollow at the base of the mountain. The desperate travelers secured help from another train and marched a hundred strong against the hiding place. The Ute scattered and fled across the ridges, leaving the stock to be recaptured. This was the "battle" of Battle Mountain, and it shows how mild were the encounters with hostile Indians when such a minor incident would be so remembered.

15 The Whitman Massacre

W HEN MARCUS WHITMAN established his mission on the Walla Walla River among the Cayuse tribe, he found most of the Indians indifferent to his teachings. Unlike the Nez Perce, they had no great desire to learn to read and write or to join Whitman's church. Eventually they became a bit disturbed as the mission farm increased in size and more white people came to live at the mission.

As the tide of travel swelled along the Oregon Trail, the Whitman mission became an important way station, the only one beyond Fort Laramie where vegetables, flour, milk, and butter could be bought. Dr. Whitman also treated the sick and supplied them with medicine. After dangers and hardships of the Idaho desert cross-

107

ing, followed by the toilsome climb over the Blue Mountains, the mission oasis looked like a glimpse of the Promised Land to the weary travelers.

Encouraged by the missionaries' success with cattle, both the Nez Perce and Walla Walla tribes started to build up herds of their own. When a trading party of Walla Walla went to Sacramento in 1845 to buy some cattle from the ranches there, a white ruffian murdered the son of the Walla Walla chief and stole two mules the young man owned. When the chief went to Whitman and demanded that the murderer be punished, he was further angered to learn that Whitman could do nothing because the crime had been committed in what then was Mexico, a foreign country. To the Indians this was new evidence that while the law might protect a white man against an Indian, it would not protect the Indian from the white man.

Then the Cayuse began to object to the increase of people at the mission. Along the trail, disease and accidents took their toll. At times a wagon would arrive at the mission with only the remnants of a family. Sometimes such survivors would rest for a while, planning to go on later. In a few cases they remained for months. Then some of the mountain men brought their half-Indian children into the mission to be raised and educated. In these ways the mission population increased until in 1847 there were about seventy-five people living there, as many as in an ordinary Nez Perce or Cayuse village.

In 1847 one of the wagon trains brought in a no-good

Indian from Maine, Joe Lewis, who was taken in and cared for by Dr. Whitman. In return, Lewis did his best to stir up resentment against the Whitmans, urging the Cayuse to attack them and take over the mission buildings, stock, and farmlands for themselves. He said that unless the Cayuse took drastic action soon, the mission would keep growing, taking Indian lands for new farms. When the whites felt strong enough, Lewis said, they would drive out or kill off all the Indians. Meanwhile, the whites would continue giving diseases to the Indians. When the Indians fell ill, Dr. Whitman would give them poison, instead of medicine, and they would soon die.

The poison story was aggravated by the stupid behavior of one of the mission workers, William Gray. Wanting to keep the Indians out of his melon patch, he plugged some of the melons with ipecac, an emetic but not a poison. Of course, the Indians knew at once Gray was tampering with the melons and feared that he had used strychnine, which he had been using against wolves.

In that same summer of 1847 the wagon trains brought in a very strong strain of measles, which soon became epidemic among the Cayuse. Many died in spite of the ministrations of Dr. Whitman, while white patients, seemingly just as sick, recovered under like treatment. The Cayuse began to believe that Joe Lewis was right. The whites were given good medicine while the Indians were given poison.

All these troubles and many more piled up until the Cayuse resorted to violence in an attempt to solve their problems. A small number of them attacked the mission, killing Dr. Whitman, Narcissa Whitman, and twelve of the men working with them. Several other men escaped. Forty-six women and children, unharmed, were taken to Fort Walla Walla and then down the Columbia by Hudson's Bay Company men. Frightened by the massacre and by turmoil in the other tribes, missionaries closed their missions among the Nez Perce and Spokane and went down the river, too.

The Whitman massacre came as a terrible shock to the people in the east, who had no knowledge of the many problems involved. In the Willamette Valley the settlers moved quickly to punish the Cayuse before other tribes could take up arms against the whites. They raised a volunteer army which marched to Walla Walla, but by then the guilty Indians had hidden in the mountains. All the peaceful Cayuse stayed in their villages, expecting no harm because they had done nothing wrong, but they suffered all the punishment. A few were killed, their horses and cattle stolen, and their supplies of food confiscated or destroyed. This attack, following the 1847 epidemic, left the Cayuse weak and disorganized.

In 1855 the remnants were placed on a reservation with the Umatilla and Walla Walla tribes and were gradually absorbed by them. With the disappearance of the Cayuse as a tribe, the name was given to the Western range-raised horse, which has since been known as the cayuse. Few Western people today remember that this was once the name of a proud, respected people.

110

16 The Gold Rush Problems

IN JANUARY, 1848, rich deposits of placer gold were found in the Central Valley of California, an event of great importance in Western history. Soon 100,000 treasure seekers were scouring every gravel bar and stream bed for new gold deposits, with many spectacular new strikes, each bringing a stampede of miners to the spot. Once gold was found, a wilderness area with only a few scattered Indian hunters could, in a few weeks, become a roaring mining camp with thousands of newcomers.

This was no slow encroachment on Indian lands, with a farm here and a small village there. It was an alien swarm coming in one wild rush, outnumbering the local Indian men 10 or 20 to 1, making armed resistance

111

hopeless. And for the most part, the mining camps were far from the Indian villages, thus reducing the initial friction between the two cultures. It is of interest to note that there is no record of an organized Indian attack against any mining camp, although on occasion a large party of armed warriors might ride up to the outskirts with some protest. Small parties of prospectors were subject to attack, and some of them far from the main camps were wiped out.

The miners filled the placer districts of the whole Great Basin and Plateau, in one big rush, the first rich strike being at Virginia City, Nevada, in 1859, the last at Silver City, Idaho, in 1864, a span of five years. Each strike followed the same general pattern. After the first rush, many disappointed men turned to supplying the miners with meat from wild game, while others started small gardens and farms to furnish vegetables, butter, milk, and eggs to the ready market.

At first the local Indians found the miners would buy any food the Indians could furnish and would take all the extra horses at a good price. But in a short time market hunters ranged the hills, slaughtering the game, farmers encroached on desirable land, and the Indians suffered from new diseases and too much whiskey. By the time the red men discovered the dangers they had been weakened beyond the point of offering effective resistance.

On one occasion at Pyramid Lake, in Nevada, the miners did goad the Indians into resistance. In 1860 a party of whites managed to capture some Indian women and took them back to town to do domestic chores. When the Indian men discovered what had happened, they raised a force of about 100 men and rescued the women, their show of force and rapidity of action so intimidating the miners that there was no fighting. The whites considered this action by the Indians an outrage which had to be punished. About the same time some other Indians made a few small raids on scattered farms in western Nevada and northeastern California, stealing some stock, killing one man, and burning his cabin.

The miners decided to wipe out the entire Indian camp on the shore of Pyramid Lake. They gathered 105 volunteers and marched out on May 9, only to walk into a well-set ambush. About half the volunteers escaped by a mad dash to the rear. The rest were killed on the spot, most by arrows, for these poverty-stricken Indians could not afford many guns.

Following this fight, white volunteers spent some time each summer hunting Indian villages to attack. The summer of 1866 brought the most success, with 172 Indians being killed in their villages throughout northwestern Nevada. Of this imposing number, at least 100 were women and children, for these volunteers took no prisoners and left no survivors.

17 Treaties and Wars of the 1850's

IN 1849 the federal government decided on a new approach to the Indian problem. The Bureau of Indian Affairs was taken from the War Department and placed in the newly created Department of the Interior. Up to that time most of the Indian troubles had been east of the Mississippi River, as the Indians were crowded onto smaller and smaller reservations or were removed bodily to Oklahoma to make way for more farmers. Then, with the acquisition of Texas in 1845, the Oregon boundary settlement in 1846, and the treaty with Mexico in 1848, the United States acquired well over 100,000 more Indians.

With the rush of new settlers to the West, trouble with the Indians developed along the overland trails. The

Indian Bureau believed that the amount and severity of conflict between the two groups could be greatly reduced if the Indians could be persuaded to mark out the boundaries of their tribal lands and then stay within them. This would open up wide corridors between tribal holdings for emigrant trains, freighting outfits, and stagecoach lines. In critical areas where there was no corridor or where two tribes each claimed the same land, the federal government would buy up the tribal rights for the necessary strip.

Roving war parties presented the most serious problem. These fighting men were out looking for excitement and could mount an attack at a moment's notice. Any person or group they chanced to meet was considered fair game. Any plan which would keep these men at home would go far toward making the trails safe and would increase the profits and lessen the risks of traders dealing with the tribes.

It was expected that several of the tribes would look at the extensive tribal holdings and decide they did not really need that much land, for they had lost a large portion of their people by disease. The remnants of a tribe migh prefer payments in goods and services, rather than the possession of surplus land. This new policy proved fairly successful, although some of the tribes later regretted having sold any of their ancient holdings once the white settlers hemmed them in.

In the Columbia Basin the first treaty council was held in the Walla Walla Valley in May and June, 1855.

Isaac Stevens, sent out as the first governor of the newly created Washington Territory, called for the leaders of many tribes to meet with him so he could explain the new program to them. He pointed out that any of the tribes signing such a treaty would receive payments in clothes, blankets, tools, farm implements, and other goods. Also, schools, hospitals, blacksmith and carpenter shops, and other facilities would be built on each reservation.

After a long and often stormy series of meetings, the council finally agreed on a number of reservations and set the value in dollars, with a schedule of payments, on the land surrendered. The Umatilla, Walla Walla, and Cayuse tribes were put together on one reservation on the Umatilla River, the Yakima and Palouse on another reservation on the Yakima River, and the Nez Perce on a third on the Snake, Clearwater, and Salmon rivers. Later the Spokane were given a reservation north of the Spokane River, and the Coeur d'Alene received one near Coeur d'Alene Lake.

As soon as the chiefs had signed the treaties, interested white men insisted that they had a right to move into the lands which the Indians had promised to sell. The same whites also claimed the right to cross the reservations any time they wished, although the treaties contained no such provisions but gave the tribes explicit authority to prevent such passage. The Indians also thought the treaties were in force and began asking for the promised payments. However, the treaties were not binding on the federal government until they had been accepted by the Senate. A private quarrel of long standing between Governor Isaac Stevens and General John E. Wool, commanding the U.S. Army forces in the Northwest, led each to oppose the other on every facet of the Indian question. As a result, the Senate delayed action for four years, and no payments reached the tribes until 1860.

The big gold rush reached the Columbia Basin across the line in British Columbia just after the treaties were written. Hordes of prospectors flocked in, ignoring the reservation boundaries as they searched each gulch, stream bed, and gravel bar for gold. When the Indian guards opposed the invasion, the miners tried to force their way through, and in about six weeks several miners and an Indian agent were killed. Other miners were stripped of all their supplies and horses and sent back down the river, while yet others heeded the warnings and turned back without a struggle.

Troops were sent to punish the Indians for trying to protect their lands and spent a few months chasing the elusive red men along the eastern slopes of the Cascades. When General Wool refused to send troops at the request of Governor Stevens, the latter raised several companies of volunteers, including one cavalry troop of Nez Perce, and a scout troop of forty more, all furnishing their own horses, in addition to supplying several hundred for the rest of the army.

The several skirmishes between the Indians and the troops were fought on Yakima lands, so this outbreak

117

is often called the Yakima War. It finally ended when the weary troops returned to their posts with nothing accomplished toward settling the problems.

An overflow of miners from the Cariboo district in southeastern British Columbia worked their way down the Columbia and crossed the border into northeastern Washington. There again the Indians turned out to repel the invasion. Then parties of whites trying to reach the upper Okanogan country by following up the east bank of the Columbia were attacked on at least three occasions, and some of them were killed.

In May, 1858, the Army decided to send Colonel Edward J. Steptoe from new Fort Walla Walla north to Spokane Falls and on to Colville to investigate reports of troubles and to hunt for some Palouse Indians who had stolen some stock from the fort. Steptoe took a force of 158 men, most of them armed with smoothbore musketoons, effective only at short range. Then the packers for the column left some of the ammunition behind in order to carry more food.

Thirty miles south of the Spokane River Colonel Steptoe's path was blocked by a large force of Coeur d'Alene, Spokane, and small groups from several other tribes. When the Indians ordered Steptoe to turn back, he moved forward to Pine Creek instead. The next morning fighting broke out between the two forces. Steptoe retreated slowly, hunting for a good place to make a stand while mounted Indians dashed about on all sides just out of range of the musketoons, while their own guns killed several horses and a soldier.

Finally, the troops reached a hilltop, far from water. There they fought off the Indians all that long day, firing about 4,000 rounds of ammunition from the musketoons with little effect beyond the smoke and noise. Some Indians were killed and wounded when they tried to drag away the body of an officer and a hand-to-hand fight ensued.

When night came, the warriors withdrew. The troops piled up all their supplies, two mountain howitzers, and some odds and ends. They abandoned several horses in poor condition. Then, leaving their campfires burning, they slipped off to the south and made a dash for the Red Wolf crossing on the Snake 60 miles away. Along the way they abandoned two badly wounded men. At the crossing, with help from the Nez Perce village, they ferried the river and returned to Fort Walla Walla.

The Army then ordered Colonel George Wright to take 400 men and go out to punish the Indians. Wright's men were supplied with the new rifled muskets, which had an effective range of 400 yards, about five times that of Steptoe's musketoons. Wright drilled his men well and put them out on the firing range with the new guns until they were convinced they had fine weapons. Then he marched north from Fort Walla Walla to the Spokane country.

The same hostile band turned out in force to attack but soon broke and ran from the deadly fire of the new rifles, which outranged their own guns by about 200 yards. This was the Battle of Four Lakes, fought on September 1. Four days later the Indians lost a skirmish on

119

Spokane Plains, and the war was over. Colonel Wright captured and slaughtered 850 horses and hanged several warriors. At about the same time Major Robert Garnett caught several Indians along the Columbia near the site of Indian attacks on mining parties and shot the captives. This ended serious Indian resistance in the Columbia Basin for nineteen years.

18 The Nez Perce and the Gold Rush

THE GOLD RUSH into Nez Perce lands demonstrated that even an intelligent, friendly cooperative Indian tribe had no way of stemming the rush of outsiders, nor could such a tribe adjust rapidly enough to the white man's ways to avoid disaster. In this case the clash be-between the cultures is in sharp focus, for there were no raids, skirmishes, or atrocities to distract the attention and to stir up emotional reactions.

Like the Yakima, the Nez Perce put guards on their trails to keep out prospectors and succeeded in turning back several groups. Finally, in midsummer, 1860, a few men managed to slip by well to the north of the main trail. They soon discovered gold on the Orofino Creek a few miles north of the Weippe camas meadows.

The Nez Perce found the mining camp almost at once, but they were not alarmed. The miners were few in number and working far from the camas grounds and pasturelands. Also, the miners asked for any fish, meat, fruit, and vegetables the Nez Perce had for sale and offered good prices for such supplies. This friendly relationship continued through the winter to the satisfaction of both groups.

But in the spring one of the miners went down the Columbia with a poke of gold dust and a report that the Nez Perce were friendly. This brought a wild rush of treasure hunters swarming up the Snake River, to unload from the boats at the mouth of the Clearwater. Many more came across the old trail from Walla Walla to the same spot. The alarmed Nez Perce called on their agent to bring in the soldiers to protect the tribe against this invasion. Although the Treaty of 1855 had promised such help, the agent could find no troops for the task. It was futile to ask the Army commander at Fort Vancouver for soldiers for such duty. Agent A. J. Cain advised the Nez Perce chiefs to hold a friendly council with the whites and try to reach some sort of formal agreement on the problem, thus avoiding possible fighting.

The Nez Perce came to the council and agreed that the miners could prospect and mine freely north of the main Clearwater, but none was to cross over to the south bank. Then the steamboat operators pointed out that the only suitable place to unload their boats was on the east bank of the Snake, just south of the mouth of the Clearwater. So the Nez Perce gave special permission for a wharf and a warehouse there, with the firm promise by the whites that none of them would live south of the Clearwater.

As soon as the Nez Perce left, the whites occupied the south bank in such numbers that they soon had a tent city of 1,500 people, with more permanent structures being built as fast as building materials could be obtained. This soon grew into Lewiston, Idaho.

Next, large numbers of newcomers to the mining camp on the Orofino Creek, finding no place to stake their claims, formed an armed party of 200 men to force their way across the Clearwater to prospect up the South Fork. The Nez Perce did not attack them, and soon the prospectors had made rich new discoveries at Elk City and Florence. The news of these rich strikes brought in a new swarm of eager men.

By that time the whole Nez Perce country was in such turmoil that there was no way to uphold the Indian rights under the Treaty of 1855. The federal officials decided the treaty should be canceled since it could not be enforced. They proposed cutting down the Nez Perce reservation, leaving out all the goldfields and the area around Lewiston. In the summer of 1863, after bitter opposition by many of the Nez Perce leaders, the new treaty was signed by the chiefs who lived around Lapwai and Kamiah and whose lands were included in the new, smaller reservation. Chiefs whose bands lived outside the new boundaries would not sign, for the treaty would confiscate all their lands. The federal officials insisted that the treaty was binding on the whole tribe, even though it had been approved by a minority group. In addition to being less than half the tribe, it was a well-defined group.

This fight over the Treaty of 1863 divided the Nez Perce into two groups: the treaty Indians on the reservation and the nontreaty bands still living outside the new boundary but on the lands guaranteed them by the Treaty of 1855. Once the treaty had been signed by some of the Nez Perce leaders, federal officials insisted that it was in effect and that whites could move into the relinquished lands at once. While the Nez Perce watched this new wave of settlement, they had nothing to show for their lost lands, for the U.S. Senate, in characteristic fashion, delayed the ratification, hence the payments, for four years.

19 Indian Wars

NEW TROUBLE was stirred up on all the Indian reservations of the United States by developments in national politics. In 1869 President Ulysses S. Grant put many excess Army officers to work as Indian agents so that they need not return to civilian life. This was unconstitutional, and after a long fight Grant was forced to remove the officers from the agency posts. About the same time a big scandal on graft in the Indian Bureau made matters worse. Grant, finally giving in to a group of church people, allowed various church bodies to nominate the agents for many of the reservations.

The Army officers had been accepted by the Indians because these men seldom tried to interfere with Indian social customs. The officers were friendly with the local businessmen, tolerating some graft or even helping defraud the Indians for a cut in the profits. Too, these officers usually were on good terms with the officers of the local Army post and could count on military help in time of trouble.

The agents nominated by the church groups annoyed the Indians by attempting to reform the red men, sometimes using strong pressure. They clashed with the local businessmen over orders for supplies and usually disagreed with the local Army officers on the best way to handle Indians. All these items were factors in a series of Indian hostilities in the 1870's.

Many of the Army officers, including the commanding general, William T. Sherman, stated that the best solution for the whole Indian problem was to kill them all. The slogan of this group was: "The only good Indian is a dead Indian." Since the American people would not permit the Army to exterminate the tribes, the Army planned to put all the stray bands on reservations and take away their horses, thus making it difficult for the warriors to slip off on raids against whites or other Indians. Starting about 1870, the Indian Bureau, with Army backing, began rounding up the strays throughout the West.

In southern Oregon a small band of Modoc was placed on the Klamath Reservation among their enemies, the Klamath. The agent even encouraged the Klamath to pick quarrels with the Modoc and to steal from them. The Modoc soon tired of this treatment. In order to escape slow destruction, they moved away to an unsettled area outside the reservation. When a volunteer posse of whites went out to attack the Modoc camp, they were driven off with some loss.

The frightened defeated volunteers called for the Army to come to the rescue. Troops were sent to chase the Modoc, who took refuge in the rough lava beds just across the line in California. There a force of about 45 Modoc fighting men, burdened with their families, held off an army of 1,800 for several weeks, killing 47 soldiers, 16 volunteers, 2 scouts, and 18 settlers. The Modocs lost 5, and 2 of these were blown up playing with a dynamite bomb dropped into their hideout. Finally, the Indians quarreled among themselves and were captured easily when they left the shelter of the lava beds. This was in 1873.

The news of the fight spread rapidly through the restless tribes of the West. Since the Modoc had no reputation among their fellow Indians as fighters, many tribes thought that if the Modoc could do that well against soldiers, surely a large number of the best warriors could wipe out any force sent against them. The Sioux began planning a great federation of several thousand warriors to kill off the whole U.S. Army. They fell far short of their goal in signing up allies and reached the peak of their success when they wiped out Custer and most of the Seventh Cavalry at the Little Bighorn in 1876. The American people were deeply shocked by Custer's defeat and blamed both the Army high command and the Indian Bureau for allowing the Indians to assemble such a force. To prevent a recurrence of the Indian success, more Indian bands were to be put on reservations under closer watch. High on the list of these bands was that led by Chief Joseph, a Nez Perce who lived in the Wallowa country of northeastern Oregon. His was a wealthy band, pasturing thousands of horses and cattle on a million acres of land.

Chief Joseph had made such a strong protest against the Treaty of 1863 that President Grant, in 1873, set aside a large part of the Wallowa country for the Indians. Then, under heavy pressure from Oregon officials, Grant canceled this order in 1875. After more meetings and arguments, General Oliver O. Howard, in command of all Army troops in the Northwest, called all the Nez Perce chiefs to a meeting at Lapwai in May, 1877. At the meeting Howard gave strict orders that all the non-treaty bands must be on the reservation with all their stock within thirty days or their villages would be attacked by the cavalry. It meant that the Wallowa band must swim all their herds, with the spring calves and colts, across both the Snake and the Salmon rivers, then at the height of the spring flood.

By a great effort Chief Joseph's people rounded up most of their stock and crossed the two rivers to camp at Lake Tolo on Camas Prairie about four miles west of present-day Grangeville, Idaho. Although they lost no people in the swirling floods in the deep canyons, they watched most of their cattle drown in the icy torrents.

All the Salmon River bands and several hundred other Indians were also camped at Lake Tolo, visiting, feasting, racing horses, playing stick games, their last such gathering before they went to live in the shadow of the agency with its domineering agent. Then, suddenly, the peaceful scene was shattered by a few young men from the Salmon River who rode out to avenge the deaths of some relatives murdered by settlers within the previous three years.

News of the raid threw the whole Northwest into an uproar. Frantic settlers 100 miles or more away huddled in their small villages expecting an attack at any moment. In this crisis General Howard acted quickly. He ordered two companies of cavalry under Captain David Perry to march out from Fort Lapwai to wipe out the entire Indian camp.

After the raid, the Nez Perce scattered from Lake Tolo. Many went to villages on the reservation. The Wallowa band, except for Chief Joseph and his family, joined Chief Looking Glass on the Clearwater. Chief Joseph went with the Salmon River bands south across the ridge to White Bird Creek.

Captain Perry and his men rode out late in the evening from Fort Lapwai in a steady rain. They rode all night and all the next day except for brief stops for breakfast and supper.

In the Indian camp at White Bird were about 50 fighting men, besides a few older men who could fight a little in defense of the camp. The Nez Perce, deciding they should try to talk peace with the soldiers, sent out a man with a flag of truce to meet Captain Perry and propose a council.

Captain Perry's troops, 100 strong, came down the open valley in column of fours, with a picket guard a quarter of a mile in advance and 11 volunteers riding with Perry at the middle of the column. The picket guard topped a small ridge and saw the Nez Perce camp beyond and an Indian walking toward them waving a white flag. An Army scout shot at the flag-bearer, and the Nez Perce War had begun.

Perry had time to choose his ground. He dismounted the 11 volunteers, placing them in some rocks on the left. Then Company F dismounted and formed a skirmish line, with the horses to the rear. Company H rode up at a sharp trot and deployed, still mounted, on the right.

Against this Army force of 111 men the Nez Perce could muster 65, not all of them classed as warriors, and some armed only with bows and arrows or muzzle-loading guns. Fifteen Nez Perce charged Perry's left wing at a sharp gallop, shooting as they came. They wounded 2 volunteers and put the rest to flight, then turned against the flank of the skirmish line. At that moment 50 Indians charged from the right against Company H. The entire line broke in panic. Some of the skirmishers reached their horses and rode to safety. Nineteen were trapped on foot and killed. The victorious Nez Perce secured several horses, sixty-three guns, and a supply of ammunition. Perry's losses totaled 34 killed, 4 wounded. The Nez Perce had 2 wounded.

Here was no great strategy, no military genius, no ambush. The fight was won by hard-riding, straight-shooting Indians who charged soldiers drawn up ready to receive them on an open field.

130

The White Bird defeat brought consternation to the Army. The Modoc success could be explained away by stressing the natural fortress of the lava beds, and Custer went down before a massed attack of the great Sioux warriors. But at White Bird an Army force, choosing its own field and lined up for battle, was crushed in a few minutes by a Nez Perce force a little more than half its size. General Howard was forced to act quickly to rebuild Army prestige and to prevent all the restless, discontented Indians in the Columbia Basin from flocking into the Nez Perce camp.

The proud Nez Perce, knowing Howard would attack again with new forces, decided that when he approached, they would cross the Salmon. If Howard crossed, too, the Nez Perce would come back at once and move off toward Kamiah.

In a few days General Howard had collected a force of 400 men at Fort Lapwai and moved out to the White Bird battlefield to bury the dead. Then he went on to the Salmon and crossed, taking two days where the Nez Perce had taken two hours, for Howard needed boats for his troops and supplies. When he had followed the Nez Perce trail 25 miles down stream, he came to another river crossing, but there he had no boats and could not follow the fleeing red men. He had to backtrack to the boats at the White Bird crossing.

Once across the Salmon the second time, the Nez Perce were safe for a few days from General Howard. But Captain Perry was at Cottonwood with 120 men, about double the Indian fighting force, and right across the path to the east. The Nez Perce wiped out a scouting party of 11 cavalry. Then their young scouts had a running fight with a band of 17 volunteers from Mount Idaho, killing 4 while losing 1 of their own.

While Captain Perry and his men stayed securely in their rifle pits at Cottonwood, the entire Nez Perce band —women, children, pack strings, and spare horses— moved across the open prairie two miles away in plain sight of the troops who did not dare come out and face the guard of 70 warriors.

Meanwhile, General Howard had ordered an attack on the peaceful village of Chief Looking Glass at the forks of the Clearwater. A hasty shot from the advancing troops warned the camp, and only 4 Indians died in the attack but they left all their tipis, supplies, and many of their horses in the rush to escape. General Howard expressed surprise that the attack sent Chief Looking Glass with his band to join the hostile bands then camped at the mouth of Cottonwood Creek.

There the hostile Nez Perce reached their largest number of fighting men—about 150, with some 550 non-combatants. A hundred tipis sheltered the band, with a family of 6 to 8 in each.

A party of volunteers from Grangeville approached the Nez Perce camp across the rolling prairie to the west, looking for Indian horses to capture. They found some, but the Nez Perce chased the raiders, cornering them on a high grassy butte and holding them there all night. In the morning both the Nez Perce and all the good horses were gone, and the butte had a new name, Fort Misery. The Nez Perce kept watch to the west, expecting General Howard to approach along the path of the retreating raiders.

While the Nez Perce rested and waited at the mouth of Cottonwood Creek, Howard crossed the South Fork several miles up stream and moved north along the open prairie on the Plateau east of the Indian camp. An officer rode to the valley rim for a view of the country and was surprised to see the large camp in the river bottom with some of the Indians bathing in the river and others holding horse races. The Nez Perce were surprised in turn when Howard opened fire on the camp with a howitzer from the rim.

After a hasty run for guns and horses, the men formed in three groups. About 75 guarded the downstream approach, a like number held the upstream side, while 24 volunteers followed old Toohoolhoolzote, the noted fighter, across the South Fork and up the steep slope to the valley rim. There they formed a skirmish line in the grass, and somewhat to their surprise halted Howard's 400 men in their tracks. The troops piled their baggage, put their horses around the pile, and formed a protecting ring around the whole with hastily dug rifle pits. Once the Nez Perce knew the camp was safe from immediate assault, more men came up and joined the skirmish line. About 75 Indians held at bay over 400 troops who did not even dare go to a nearby spring to quench their thirst.

The next day a pack string with ammunition and a guard of soldiers joined Howard, giving him about 580

133

men. By this time several of the Nez Perce had decided that they had nothing more to gain by the sniping and had gone back to camp. Howard was able to move out against the few remaining warriors. He captured the spring and advanced on the camp.

The Nez Perce fled from the camp in some confusion, leaving tipis and belongings. They crossed the ridge to Kamiah, forded the Clearwater, and went into camp at Weippe. Then they held a council, for the Indians now realized that they could not go on from day to day but needed some long-range plan.

Now that General Howard's troops outnumbered the warriors more than 4 to 1, and many more soldiers were on the way to join him, the chiefs decided it would be futile to turn back for another fight. Chief Joseph said that if they would not fight for their homes, they all should surrender, but he was voted down. The council decided they would cross the mountains to the buffalo country, leaving their war with General Howard in Idaho. They had no idea they were at war with the whole U.S. Army.

Then the great retreat began. Its success did not depend on the genius of a great leader, but on the cooperation of close-knit family groups who were very intelligent and had a large number of superior horses. Among these fine animals the Appaloosas were rated highly for their endurance, the toughness of their hooves, and their ability to thrive on scanty feed.

Each family group lived in its own tipi, managed its own horses and packs, and moved as a unit. Each person, even a small child, had his own riding horse. Also, each person needed a pack horse and a spare. Since there were 700 Nez Perce, it meant about 2,000 horses had to move through the mountains, often along narrow trails.

Each morning each family turned out promptly and went to work. While one prepared the breakfast, others brought in and saddled the horses, and still others tied up the packs. There was much bustle and scurrying around, with little confusion. In half an hour or so, breakfast was eaten, the packs were loaded, and each person mounted his own horse. Then they moved in a body out along the trail, with their spare horses and all their gear. They took their place in the long line of other small family groups, and the entire camp of 700 was soon in orderly motion. After five to eight hours of traveling they stopped, set up camp, and turned the horses out to graze and rest until the next morning.

Along the crest of the high, rough mountain ridge of the Lolo Trail they went, through Lolo Pass and down Lolo Creek, where they found the narrow valley floor blocked by a small log fort manned by about 30 soldiers and more than 100 settlers. Most of the settlers had been friends of these same Nez Perce for years, visiting and trading with the Indians as they traveled back and forth to the buffalo country.

When these trustworthy Nez Perce said, "Let us go through your land in peace. There has never been a quarrel between us," the settlers obliged. While Captain Charles Rawn sat helpless in his little fort, the whole body of Indians rode past along the mountainside to the north and on to Stevensville, where they bought food and clothing. Then they moved a few miles south and held another council to choose their path.

Three paths lay open to them. Chief Joseph favored returning by the Lolo Trail and surrendering. Others wanted to go northeast across the mountains on the short road to the Canadian plains in Alberta. Chief Looking Glass persuaded the council they should choose the third path, south up the Bitterroot Valley, across to Yellowstone Park and on east to central Wyoming to join their friends, the Crows.

A hundred miles to the south, across the Continental Divide, they came to the North Fork of the Big Hole River. There they made camp in a large meadow with a few clumps of willows along the banks of the stream and heavy timber on the hills. They cut and dried lodgepoles, while the horses pastured and rested in the great meadow.

A few white scouts rode by on the hills. The Indians knew the war was over, so they ignored these visitors. But General Howard was still following their trail, and ahead of him Colonel John Gibbon hastened up the Bitterroot Valley with 160 soldiers and 45 volunteers, hot on the fresh trail.

In the gray dawn of August 9, with wisps of fog hanging above the stream, Gibbon launched a surprise attack against the sleeping camp, killing about 50 women and children in their beds or as they stumbled from their tipis. Most of the men managed to grab their guns and reached the willow thickets, but 30 fell in the fierce fighting that followed.

Then the troops, thinking the fighting was over, set fire to the lodges, too wet with dew to burn. Soon the warriors opened a deadly fire from the willows and forced the troops out of the camp. They retreated to a wooded knoll and dug in.

The Nez Perce kept up a sharp fire, holding Gibbon and his men in their rifle pits while the rest of the band buried their dead. Then they struck camp and moved off to the south, leaving the warriors to continue the fight.

After a hectic day and a long night under heavy fire, Gibbon was rescued by the arrival of General Howard. While the weary troops rested and bound up their wounds, Howard's Bannock scouts were permitted to dig up the Nez Perce dead and strip the bodies of their blankets, clothing, and scalps. The surprise attack on the camp, the presence of Stevensville volunteers with Gibbon, and the desecration of the dead embittered the Nez Perce and convinced them that all whites were enemies. For the rest of the war they attacked some of the ranches along their path and knocked over freight trains and stagecoaches, in addition to fighting soldiers and scouts.

The Nez Perce fled south into Idaho and turned east toward Yellowstone Park. Meanwhile, Howard had found fresh horses and followed rapidly, cutting across Monida Pass. At Camas Creek he was only a few miles behind the Indians who were annoyed at his close pursuit. To slow Howard down, they organized a night raid on the Army camp and made off with 173 pack mules, delaying Howard's march for several days until he could build up a new pack string and secure more supplies.

The fleeing Nez Perce crossed Yellowstone Park and the Wyoming mountains to the Crow country, only to find they were not welcome there. They turned north to seek safety in Canada 300 miles away. As they came out of the mountains they managed to elude a new army under Colonel Samuel D. Sturgis, who had come south from Yellowstone Valley. The chagrined Sturgis followed in hot pursuit and fought a skirmish with the Nez Perce rear guard at Canyon Creek north of the Yellowstone, where a few Indian riflemen held back the troops until the families and horse herd were safely up the canyon and out on the open plains beyond.

When General Howard found that the Nez Perce were easily running away from Sturgis and his fresh cavalry, he ordered out still another army force from Fort Keogh. Led by Colonel Nelson A. Miles, these fresh troops rode north to the Missouri, crossed at the mouth of the Musselshell, and dashed to the west to cut off the fugitives.

Ignorant of this new danger, the Nez Perce moved north across their old hunting grounds to the Cow Island crossing on the Missouri, where steamboats had unloaded 200 tons of supplies for the Montana mining camps. The Nez Perce helped themselves to free groceries, clothing, and other supplies while the small guard of soldiers prudently stayed on a hill some distance away. Then the Indians moved north up Cow Creek, around the eastern flank of the Bear Paw Mountains, and camped in a shallow coulee on Snake Creek, where they rested a few days while the hunters killed buffalo for winter meat and robes.

On a dreary morning in late September, Colonel Miles with about 600 soldiers, packers, and Indian scouts, approached the camp across the open prairie, hoping to wipe out the entire camp with one dashing charge. The Nez Perce were caught by surprise. They were just breaking camp and packing their gear, getting ready to move across into Canada 50 miles to the north. A thin line of warriors on the coulee rim stopped the charging cavalry, leaving a line of blue-clad dead to mark the limits of the advance. Then Miles surrounded the camp and waited for help.

A chilling snowstorm blew in from the north, slowing the fighting. When General Howard arrived a few days later with more men to strengthen the line of troops on the snow-swept prairie, the Indians knew there was no hope of escape. Only half the fighting men were still alive. All the chiefs and war leaders, except Chief Joseph and Old Chief White Bird, had fallen. Each day more men, women, and children died under the hail of bullets from the soldiers' rifles, while the living huddled in wet, cold pits, worn-out and hungry. The Nez Perce had come to the end of the trail.

On the morning of October 5 the north wind had died, the clouds had broken, and the sun was shining forth. A truce was arranged, and Chief Joseph called the remnants of the Nez Perce fighters into a last council. General Howard sent one of his Nez Perce inter-preters, Captain John, to listen to the council and to bring back the decision. After a long discussion, Chief Joseph arose for his final words. He turned to Captain John and said, "Tell General Howard I know his heart. What he told me before I have in my heart. I am tired of fighting. Our chiefs are killed. Looking Glass is dead. Toohoolhoolzote is dead. The old men are all dead. It is the young men who say yes and no. He who led on the young men is dead. It is cold, and we have no blankets. The little children are freezing to death. My people, some of them, have run away to the hills and have no blankets, no food; no one knows where they are—perhaps freezing to death. I want time to look for my children and see how many I can find. Maybe I shall find them among the dead."

Then he turned to his comrades. "Hear me, my chiefs. I am tired. My heart is sick and sad. From where the sun now stands, I will fight no more forever."

Eighty-seven men, 40 of them wounded, surrendered with 184 women and 147 children. One hundred and fifty-one men, women, and children lay dead along the war trail. About 100 escaped to Canada. In the war the army had lost 126 killed, 140 wounded. The Nez Perce captives were exiled first to Kansas, then to Oklahoma.

20 Smoholla, the Dreamer

OF ALL THE prophets along the Columbia, the most important was Smoholla, of the Wanapum tribe of Shahaptin stock. He was born about 1817, near the mouth of the Snake River. When he reached adolescence, he went up in the hills on his spirit quest. After a few years of practice he was able, by self-hypnosis, to put himself into a trance which might last as long as five days. As was common among the prophets of that area, Smoholla brought back messages for the people from the Old One.

As his influence among the Indians grew, Smoholla became an object of interest to government officials. Here is his description by one of them in 1884, when Smoholla was nearly seventy:

141

In person Smoholla is peculiar. Short, thick-set, bald-headed and almost hunch-backed, he is not prepossessing at first sight, but he has an almost Websterian head, with a deep brow over bright, intelligent eyes. He is a finished orator. His manner is mostly of the bland, insinuating, persuasive style, but when aroused he is full of fire and seems to handle invective effectively. His audience seemed spellbound under his magnetic manner.

As a young man Smoholla went on several raids with war parties against other tribes. Then in his early thirties he turned to prophesying and preaching. Soon he had a substantial following and had incurred the jealousy of Chief Moses of the Mid-Columbia tribe just up the river. A hand-to-hand fight ensued, which Moses won, and left Smoholla on the riverbank presumably dying. In the night the injured man revived enough to climb into a canoe and drift down the river out of danger. When he returned a few years later, he explained that he had been in the spirit world all that time with Old One. Now he had been sent back with many messages for the Indians.

Smoholla returned at an opportune time, just as the big gold rush to Nez Perce country started. This increased the unrest among the Indians who had objected to the Treaty of 1855 and who had helped attack prospecting parties along the river. Smoholla was able to take advantage of the Indians' unrest to build up his following.

Smoholla (seated, front right, dressed in light shirt), the prophet of the Columbia River Indians, and his priests inside a lodge. Copy made in 1884; original photographer and date not recorded.

(Smithsonian Institution)

Smoholla's trances became more frequent, often during a meeting with his followers. Some skeptics thought he might be shamming, but he did not even twitch a muscle when stuck with pins, nor did he bleed from shallow cuts. His trances were so like heavy sleep that his followers considered his messages as products of his dreams; they became known as Dreamers among the white settlers.

Basically Smoholla followed closely the pattern of the

prophet cult. He taught that a terrible convulsion of nature would destroy the world; then Old One would restore the days of long ago, before the coming of the white man and would bring back to earth all the Indians who had died. If any living Indian wanted to be chosen to live in this new world, he had to follow the teachings of Smoholla, wear Indian clothes, and obey the Indian code of conduct. The Indian agents tried to counteract this as best they could by making their charges on the reservations cut their hair and wear white man's clothes.

Smoholla made one important addition to the former teachings. Old One would destroy all the white invaders when he destroyed the present earth. The whites had harmed the land, the Earth-Mother. They had torn her with plows, cut down her forests, and dug holes in her hills. Such desecration made the destruction of the whole white race a necessity if the Indians were to live at peace again according to their ancient pattern.

Although Smoholla's teachings never did stir up any outbreak along the Columbia, many of the hostile Nez Perce in the war of 1877 followed the Dreamer teachings. Later some of the teachings became the basis of the widespread Ghost Dance religion which first developed in Nevada.

21 Wovoka, the Indian Messiah

"WHEN THE SUN DIED, I went up to heaven and saw God and all the people who had died a long time ago. God told me to come back and tell my people they must be good and love one another, and not fight, or steal, or lie. He gave me this dance to give to my people."

Wovoka, the Indian messiah, thus explained the origin of the Ghost Dance doctrine and the religious movement which swept through the Indian tribes from the Sierra Nevada to the eastern edge of the Great Plains, converting several thousand Indians in a few months and causing great uneasiness among Indian Bureau officials and Army commanders.

Wovoka was born in the lowly Paviotso tribe, cousins to the neighboring Paiute, in the Mason Valley on the

145

Walker River in western Nevada about 1856. He always said he was about four years old when the Paiute fought the miners at Pyramid Lake in 1860. His father, Tavibo, was a prophet of some standing among his own people. Before he died in 1870, he had taught Wovoka some of his magic.

The Paviotso tribe were of the Digger group, living by hunting and by gathering seeds, berries, and roots. After white settlers came to the Mason Valley in the 1860's, many of the Paviotso worked for them during the summer season for very low pay.

The orphaned Wovoka was taken in by a rancher, David Wilson, who called the boy Jack, and he was known as Jack Wilson to the settlers and later to the Indian agents.

Wilson had a son, Bill, about the same age as Wovoka. The two grew up together and became fast friends, working, hunting, and fishing together for several years. The two friends depended on each other for many favors.

Wovoka had some gift for falling into light trances. This trait, together with the sleight of hand learned from his father, gave him some standing as a prophet among the Paviotso, but he wanted to increase his prestige by some remarkable deed which his fellow tribesmen could consider a miracle. Once he had made his plans, he secured the enthusiastic support of Bill Wilson.

In July the Mason Valley bakes under the desert sun, with the temperature at midday hovering around 100 degrees. Wovoka decided that if he could produce ice

Wovoka (right), or "the Cutter," also known as Jack Wilson, was the Paiute messiah, son of Tavibo, the prophet. Born in 1856, he was photographed at his home in Mason Valley, Nevada, by James Mooney in 1891.

(Smithsonian Institution)

floating in the river on such a day, the Paviotso would be impressed. He announced the ice-making attempt and set the day and the time, high noon. The Indians assembled around him on the bridge and on the river banks while he went through his incantations for an hour or so. Then, as the crowd became restless, several large chunks of ice came floating down the current to be salvaged by the excited crowd.

Of course, Wovoka really was responsible for the ice in the river, but it had come from the Wilson icehouse and had been dumped in the stream about half a mile above the bridge by Bill Wilson, an explanation which apparently never occurred to the Paviotso. This ice venture was such a success that Wovoka on a later occasion had a cake of ice drop from the sky, really from a big cottonwood tree, onto a sacred robe. This was done at night. The public success of this accomplishment, announced in advance, brought Wovoka new prestige as a prophet with great powers.

In the next few years he continued to have a few light trances and awoke from each with some new message from Old One, but his great vision did not come until fourteen years after the ice show. Late in December, 1888, he became ill, possibly with scarlet fever. While he was still an invalid in his lodge, a total eclipse blotted out the sun in the Mason Valley on January 1, 1889. All the Indians raised a loud clamor and shot off their guns in an attempt to frighten away the monster which was swallowing their sun. When they finally succeeded and the sun shone forth again, they found Wovoka had lapsed into a deep trance.

The invalid lay motionless and scarcely breathing for days. When he finally revived, he explained that he had been visiting in another world. There he had seen God and all the Indians who had died. They were happy and forever young, living in a beautiful land filled with game.

Wovoka promised his people they too could go to that pleasant other world if they would follow the rules of conduct God had sent by his messenger. They must be good, love one another, stop quarreling, put away all war practices, and live at peace with everybody, red or white. They must work to earn the things they need and not lie or steal. And several times each year they must dance, for five days at a time, using the new dance and the new songs which Wovoka had brought them.

In all this Wovoka followed closely the teachings of the prophets along the Columbia eighty years earlier. They too had gone into trances and had brought back messages after the people had been frightened by some great natural phenomenon. This whole prophet complex had been passed from tribe to tribe and had reached the Paviotso by 1870, possibly through Wovoka's father. Although these teachings resemble the Christian teachings in many ways, they had been developed before the first white man had reached the Columbia Basin.

Wovoka's great vision, following the eclipse, set the Paviotso to dancing with such fervor that news of it soon spread to other tribes, who came to watch and soon were

149

dancing, too. In two or three months the new dance had spread all over the Great Basin and to the Shoshoni and Bannock in southern Idaho, who in turn passed it along to the Wind River Shoshoni in Wyoming. Tribes from far places sent delegations to meet Wovoka and to hear his message. They went back deeply impressed. Some of them reported that they had seen their dead relatives and friends and had spoken to them. Young people in the various tribes who could read and write, having been taught in the agency schools, spread the news far and wide through letters.

With the excitement growing steadily and visiting delegations pouring into the Mason Valley, the Paviotso paid increased homage to their prophet. By this time he had the ability to go into a light trance almost at will. At almost any large gathering he would drop into a short trance, then return with a new supplementary message.

Wovoka was in such close touch with God his followers came to believe he was superhuman and would never die. Wovoka said on several occasions that he did not fear the soldiers, for any of them sent to arrest him would fall down helpless. Then one night before a large crowd of followers he stood up bare to the waist and put on a new type of cotton shirt decorated with mystic designs in red ocher. Wovoka handed a shotgun to a follower, had him move off ten paces and shoot directly at the prophet's heart. When the smoke from the black powder charge cleared away, Wovoka stood there un-

150

harmed, with a charge of buckshot scattered at his feet. The observers never seemed to suspect that the new miracle had been effected with a blank charge in the gun and buckshot from the magician's hand.

Many of the delegations, especially those from the plains, wanted shirts like the one Wovoka wore to stop the buckshot. The prophet supplied these shirts at a price and put each one on for a moment, thus giving it some of his great power. He did tell the buyers they should not do any fighting, but this part of the message was ignored. These magic shirts with the red designs soon came to be called Ghost Shirts, and the prophet's dance the Ghost Dance.

The Ghost Dance religion swept through the tribes like a prairie fire until all the plains tribes were dancing. For some reason Columbia Basin tribes were not affected, possibly because they had had Smoholla and his Dreamer teachings for a time.

Now a change was made in Wovoka's teachings. While he still insisted that the Indians should not fight the white man, he now taught that on some great day soon all the whites would be driven back across the ocean or would be drowned in a great flood, while the good Indians would go to the high mountains and be saved for the brave new world. The earth was so old and tired it needed rejuvenation before the Indians could live happily on it. In the new, better world everyone would be happy. Each spring God would make each of the Indians a year younger, so no one would ever grow old and die. In this new revelation Wovoka made a serious error rather common to prophets. He promised that all this would happen in 1891, when the grass turned green in the spring.

The Ghost Dance was an important factor leading to the tragic slaughter of the Sioux at Wounded Knee on December 29, 1890. More than 200 were slain, clad in bulletproof ghost shirts, which showed the futility of such protection against Army rifles. Even the Paviotso were shaken by the news from Wounded Knee. They had not planned to fight, but they had believed the shirts were bulletproof. When spring came and went in 1891, and none of Wovoka's prophecy came true, the whole Ghost Dance movement collapsed, but the Paviotso still believed in Wovoka as a great prophet and a great leader. Forty-one years more he lived in the Mason Valley, just plain Jack Wilson to the whites.

The Paviotso still believed Wovoka would never die. When death came to him in 1932, they were shocked. They buried him in the valley, in a grave marked with a simple headboard. Seldom has a religious leader with so great an impact on his fellowmen passed on so quietly.

22 The Bannock War of 1878

LATE IN JANUARY, 1863, General Connor defeated a band of Shoshoni at the Bear River in the hope of teaching them to leave travelers on the various trails alone. The next summer he invited the remnants of that band and other Shoshoni and Bannock to meet him in a conference at Soda Springs, Idaho. There the Indians agreed on a simple treaty, but it was never ratified by the Senate. A more comprehensive treaty was negotiated in 1868. This, together with a supplementary agreement, was accepted by Congress in 1873.

The Shoshoni and Bannock tribes agreed to a reservation, but the treaty allowed them the right to hunt and fish on any land not occupied by whites. Each year many Indians left their reservation at Fort Hall and wandered around the open desert and mountain country.

153

Then farmers began settling in the little valleys. The Indians continued to visit the same valleys to hunt and in some places to dig camas. Soon there was friction between the Indian bands trying to use their old camping grounds and the settlers who now had title to much of the land.

After a year filled with aggravating incidents the open conflict started in the Camas Valley on the Wood River drainage. An influx of settlers put herds of horses on lands the Bannock had used for summer pasture; even worse, they had turned hogs into the camas meadows. The hogs ate all the camas bulbs and ruined the whole area. An angry Indian shot a hog, a settler shot an Indian, two Indians attacked three herders, and the war was on.

Buffalo Horn, war chief of the Bannock, had won his rank in intertribal warfare. He had served also with the Crow scouts against the Sioux in 1876 and had led 30 Bannock scouts to help General Howard in the Nez Perce War. This experience convinced Buffalo Horn that Howard was a poor general. If 150 Nez Perce warriors, burdened with 400 noncombatants, could make such a showing against the Army, a much stronger force of warriors, unburdened, should be able to handle any number of soldiers General Howard might lead against them.

When the fighting started, Chief Buffalo Horn had about 150 Bannock along the Wood River. He led this force south to King's Hill on the Snake, then down the

Snake a few miles to Glen's Ferry and across the river to the Bruneau Valley. His men attacked and plundered ranches, wagon trains, and stages along the way. They slaughtered men, women, and children and in characteristic Bannock fashion mutilated the bodies. They made no pretense of following the white man's rules of war.

As Buffalo Horn had expected, the first news of the fighting brought in recruits from many places, especially from the Paiute and the tribes in the Columbia Basin. In a few weeks the chief was in command of a formidable force of several hundred men, all well supplied with arms and with plenty of spare horses captured from the plundered ranches.

As Buffalo Horn approached the Owyhee Mountains, he rode out in advance with a scouting party. They met some volunteers from the Silver City camps, who opened fire. A lucky long-range shot killed the chief, and the hostile force was left without a leader.

At the first news of hostilities General Howard was greatly alarmed. He feared a coalition of all the restless Indians in the plateau country, with another long, tough campaign. Most of all, he feared that Chief Joseph might escape from captivity in Kansas and return to lead the hostile army. Howard professed to believe that Joseph was a great military genius and that the magic of Joseph's name would bring in hundreds of new recruits. To prevent a long, costly war, Howard mustered a big army and set out in pursuit of the war party.

The war party, now numbering about 800, had no

155

effective leadership and no plan of action. Howard chased them out of southwestern Idaho and across much of eastern Oregon. When the Indians turned north, Howard had gunboats patrolling the Columbia River from Wallula to The Dalles to prevent a possible crossing. As the chase continued, the formidable Indian force gradually broke up into many smaller groups, and these in turn scattered as the individual Indians sought safety back on their reservations.

With no Indians to chase, the troops turned their attention to small groups of Bannock and Shoshoni left in southeastern Idaho and Wyoming when the men went off to war. The soldiers found a few small camps to attack. Hence, most of the casualties of the Bannock War were women and children on both sides.

23 Ute Troubles to 1880

In 1850 most of the Ute lived in western Colorado and traded at Taos and Santa Fe to the south. They crossed the mountains into eastern Colorado and north-eastern New Mexico each year to hunt buffalo for a supply of robes and dried meat, but they still had to rely on their own game and their small gardens for much of their food. They were not powerful enough to establish a permanent hold on any of the country east of the mountains, where they had many fights with the Plains tribes.

Two of the smaller Ute bands lived in eastern Utah and ranged west into Nevada until Mormon farmers moved in. The two bands gave up eastern Utah with little opposition and moved east into Colorado, where the tribe had more land than it could use. There they were unmolested until the big mining rush to the Colorado gold and silver mines from 1858 to 1860 brought in 100,000 whites.

At this time of crisis a new leader appeared among the Ute. His name was Ouray. He was born in Taos, New Mexico, in 1833, the year of the great meteoric showers. When Ouray was a baby, his parents returned to the Ute country. In 1860, at the age of twenty-seven, Ouray took over the chieftainship of his band, the Uncompahgre, which was then much the strongest of the several Ute bands. Ouray had visited the mining camps and was appalled at the great flood of whites. From then on he consistently favored peace treaties, rather than war with the whites, for he knew the Ute could not hope to win such a struggle.

In 1863, with the country in the throes of the Civil War, Chief Ouray was able to negotiate a very favorable treaty with the government. The Ute were given a reservation of 16,000,000 acres in a region not yet desired by the whites. This reservation was confirmed and the boundaries were more clearly defined in 1868. Then, in 1873, at the insistence of the silver miners, 4,000,000 acres in the Colorado mountains just north of New Mexico were sold back to the government at a small price.

The Ute wanted to continue their buffalo hunting east of the mountains. They also wanted to wander as they liked over their vast holdings, but the Indian Bureau wanted them to stay put in their little farming villages

158

and raise more crops, thus leaving much land for white settlers.

In 1878 a new agent, Nathan Meeker, was appointed to the White River agency high in the mountains in northwestern Colorado. Meeker had the specific task of instructing the Ute in farming and of keeping them on their farms. Meeker was a good man, with high ideals and a genuine sympathy for his Indian charges, but the changes he was trying to make were counter to the basic pattern of behavior of the Ute. They would have to give up their buffalo hunting and most of their horses in order to follow Meeker's plans.

Neither the Ute nor the agent seemed to realize at that time that the days of buffalo hunting were gone forever. This whole area of disagreement was settled the next year, 1880, by the total destruction of the southern buffalo herd, but the Ute, in 1879, still clung to the hope that their old pattern of hunting could be followed indefinitely.

The Ute, like several other tribes, held all the tribal lands in common. They liked to run large numbers of horses and some cattle on the open range. The Indian Bureau and the agent objected to this use of the land, for it kept out white settlers. Furthermore, it allowed the Ute too much freedom of movement and too easy a way to make a living. Subsistence farming of small plots, on the other hand, would pin them down and free several million acres for white settlement.

The Ute, as a tribe, owned about 4,000 acres for each

man, woman, and child. Under an allotment plan, each person would be reduced to a plot of 40 acres. Then the Ute horses could be sold off, preventing any roving band of hunters from bothering white settlers and saving all that grass for the settlers' herds. Each Ute would be forced to spend most of each summer in his own fields, irrigating, weeding, and hoeing his crops under the close supervision of the agent.

Meeker had some initial success, making friends with several of the Ute. They found him a great improvement in most ways over their former agents. But they would not become farmers, even to please him, and they would not give up their horses. Meeker brought matters to a showdown by plowing up some fine pastureland near the agency. When the Indians protested that their horses would be short of feed near the houses, Meeker told them they could sell off the horses if they were short of grass for the whole herd.

The Ute responded to this suggestion with violent language and threats. In the face of this unrest, Meeker sent an appeal for troops, as he had been instructed to do if trouble loomed. When the Ute learned of the approach of the cavalry column, about a dozen of them killed Meeker and six of his agency helpers. Then they went out to Mill Creek to intercept the approaching cavalry. In the ensuing fight the soldiers lost fourteen killed and forty-three wounded. This was on September 29, 1879.

The White River agency was so remote from the nearest telegraph station that it took several days for the news to reach Washington. Meanwhile, wild rumors of a general Indian uprising, similar to that of 1876, spread through the West. The Army high command again feared that all the disgruntled Indians from the Great Basin and the Columbia Basin would hurry to join the Ute, and that they would be reinforced by restless young warriors from many of the Plains tribes. They took elaborate precautions against such a widespread outbreak by sending in an overwhelming number of troops.

Chief Ouray and his band were not involved at the White River. They lived far off to the south. Ouray did not want any war, nor did he want posses of citizens and columns of cavalry chasing down. small bands of Ute for the next several years. He was able to arrange an immediate truce, so there was no more fighting. The whole affair ended with twelve Ute being arrested and named as murderers for the agency killings, but none was ever brought to trial. The next year Chief Ouray died.

To punish the whole Ute tribe for the violence at the White River and their reluctance to settle down, the officials seized their entire Colorado holdings, about 12,000,000 acres. The tribe was then settled on two small reservations just across the line in Utah, and Colorado was open to the whites.

161

24 Chief Joseph, the "Noble Red Man"

ONCE THE CIVIL WAR was over, the whole machinery of government seemed to sag. Graft and scandals reached alarming proportions, touching officials from lowly ward heelers in small cities to members of the President's Cabinet. With the slavery issue settled, many of the growing middle class turned their attention to social and government reform. Recurring scandals in the Bureau of Indian Affairs, coupled with the spectacular Indian Wars of the 1870's, centered the attention of many of the reform groups on the plight of the American Indian.

In the late eighteenth century French intellectuals had put forth the concept of the Noble Red Man, the unspoiled child of nature, free from all the vices of the decadent French court. This concept was adopted by some American writers, led by James Fenimore Cooper. Then Henry Wadsworth Longfellow joined the group. Cooper's *Leatherstocking Tales* were widely read, but Longfellow's narrative poem "Hiawatha" reached nearly every schoolchild in America. Teachers read it aloud, students memorized lengthy passages, and many of the short passages and phrases entered the common culture as quotations. Folk songs showing the Indian in a sympathetic, romantic light are exemplified by "My Little Mohee" and "Bright Alfretta."

All the public uneasiness about the Indian Bureau scandals, the bloody wars, and the slaughter of so many women and children at the Bear River, Sand Creek, Washita, Marias River, and Big Hole needed only some central, heroic, sympathetic figure around whom the sentiment could crystallize. Greatly to his surprise, Chief Joseph of the Nez Perce became that figure.

Before the war of 1877, the Nez Perce had considered Chief Joseph a young leader, with no reputation as a fighter, and yet to win his place in the select circle of tribal leaders. But General Howard and Indian agent John Monteith rated Joseph as the most important of all the nontreaty chiefs. Joseph could talk effectively in council meetings in the presence of white dignitaries, and he led the largest and wealthiest of the nontreaty bands. General Howard's reports always gave Joseph prominent mention, so he became well known to newspaper editors around the country. Then too, Joseph's name was short, easy to spell, and easy to remember. Among many of the Eastern church groups Joseph's father, Old Chief Joseph, was remembered as one of Spalding's first two converts and one of his first two Nez Perce deacons.

During the entire War of 1877 the nontreaty bands of Nez Perce were led by a council composed of chiefs and warriors, with Joseph holding a minor position in the group. But the war news, especially that sent from General Howard's headquarters, continued to feature Joseph as the dominant leader, the Red Napoleon.

When the war ended at the Bear Paw battlefield in October, Joseph was the only chief captured. Old White Bird fled to Canada, and all the others had died fighting. Reporters and Army officers alike were favorably impressed by the personality and character of Joseph. They admired him as a leader and as a man. They gave him much of the credit for the humane behavior of the Nez Perce fighting men during the war—no torture of prisoners, no killing of the wounded, no scalping or mutilating of the dead. In this war the Regular Army and their scouts did all these things.

Chief Joseph was also a fine example of the underdog, the noble leader of a lost cause, a man to be admired, respected, and pitied as long as he lost. He was large, well built, handsome, dignified in bearing, the personification of the Noble Red Man of the poets and philosophers.

Many Americans had a deep admiration for Chief

Joseph even before the war was over. Then, when the proud chief became a captive of the Army and continued to get flattering treatment from the newspapers, he was given an unusual honor.

From the Bear Paw, Joseph and the other captives were taken first to Miles City, then to Bismarck, North Dakota, where they were held for a few days. During his stay at Bismarck, he received this invitation:

Bismarck, D.T., Nov. 21, 1877

To Joseph, Head Chief of the Nez Perces.

Sir:—Desiring to show you our kind feelings and the admiration we have for your bravery and humanity, as exhibited in your recent conflict with the forces of the United States, we most cordially invite you to dine with us at the Sheridan House, in this city. The dinner to be given at 1½ P.M. today.

Joseph accepted and attended the dinner with one of his men. Two days later the whole captive group was herded into boxcars and hauled into exile, first to Fort Leavenworth, then to Baxter Springs, Kansas, and finally to Oklahoma, which at the time was Indian Territory. During the first year of captivity about 100 of the captives died from the effects of their wounds or the hardships of the long trail or from poor living conditions. Chief Joseph's protests over their shabby treatment finally resulted in his being sent to Washington, D.C., to present the Nez Perce case directly to high government officials. There he met Bishop W. H. Hare, who published a lengthy interview with Joseph in the *North American Review* in April, 1879. This led to a rebuttal by General Howard and wide publicity for the Nez Perce.

Chief Joseph was taken East on several other occasions in the next twenty-five years. Each time he received much favorable publicity, which helped give public backing to the reformers who were pushing new laws to benefit the Indians on the reservations.

Even during his lifetime Chief Joseph became a legendary figure. Army officers, in attempts to explain the Nez Perce success in pitched battles even when badly outnumbered, insisted these successes were the result of the military genius of Chief Joseph. But a careful study of the strategy and tactics of the Nez Perce from White Bird to Bear Paw reveals that Chief Joseph had no responsibility for any of the military planning. A council of fighting men, some of them chiefs, made a few sketchy plans from time to time, and the skill and bravery of the individual fighting men did the rest. But many books still support the legend of Chief Joseph, the great military genius, the Red Napoleon.

As the admiration and favorable publicity for Chief Joseph increased, it seemed possible that he might be returned to the Wallowa country with his followers. Such a return was bitterly opposed by the white settlers there, for they feared they might be held to account for the Indian stock and other property they had confiscated. Hence each time Joseph was featured in a news story in the East, violent, vicious attacks were made on him in the local newspapers in Lewiston, Idaho, and the neighboring communities.

This wave of attacks began in 1879, following Bishop Hare's interview. Joseph then was accused of having killed people in the Salmon River raids, although the accusers knew Joseph had been many miles from the scene at the time and they knew the names of the actual killers. Each bunch of accusations were accompanied by threats to lynch Joseph if he ever did return.

While this controversy raged in the Columbia Basin, many important people became interested in the Indian problems. Prominent writers took up the cause of all Indians and produced books, of which Helen Hunt Jackson's *A Century of Dishonor* is a good example. She followed this with a romantic novel, *Ramona,* dealing with the plight of some California Indians. Writers continued to present the tragedies and injustices heaped on tribe after tribe, and eventually produced some reforms, but through all the uproar no other Indian leader ever captured the fancy of the American people as did Joseph of the Nez Perce.

25 Chief Moses of the Mid-Columbia
· Salish

MOSES WAS BORN near Wenatchee about 1829, the son of the tribal chief of the Mid-Columbia Salish who claimed the riverbanks and adjoining land up- and downstream from the mouth of the Wenatchee River. This tribe had a well-established system of village chiefs holding some authority over the people. Usually the eldest son was chosen chief after his father's death, if the son had proved his worth. He also inherited most of his father's wealth. Moses had older brothers, but they had been killed in fights with other tribes. His father fell in a fight with the Blackfeet in Montana in 1848, and his oldest brother was killed by the same tribe in 1849.

Moses and another brother were active during the

troubled times of 1856–58. They skirmished against Army detachments in the Yakima country and tried to stop any parties of armed miners who came to the tribal lands. Moses' brother was shot by one of a group of miners near Wenatchee in 1858 while he was spying on them. Soon afterward Moses led a small war party east to the Spokane country to help the allied tribes there repel the column led by Colonel Wright, but he arrived after the fighting ended and did not become seriously involved.

During this same turbulent period Moses was reported to have fought with the prophet Smoholla. His victory over the prophet and his success in the skirmishing increased Moses' prestige until his claim to the chieftainship of the Mid-Columbia Salish was unquestioned. At that time he was about thirty years old.

Moses was deeply impressed by the easy victories of Colonel Wright over the large allied forces of Indians at Four Lakes and Spokane Plains. Deciding it would be futile for his tribe to challenge the U.S. Army, he began to cultivate the friendship of influential white men, and had some of them write letters for him to the Army officers. Some of the letters were sent to General Howard in the 1870's, and others went directly to the newspapers. In all these letters Moses emphasized his desire for peace with the whites.

When the Nez Perce War broke out in 1877, many of the settlers feared that Moses would collect his own men and a large number of allies from neighboring

169

bands and join in the fighting. At the time Moses could have collected from his own tribe more than double the number of warriors of all the nontreaty Nez Perce, but he had no real interest in the conflict. He might have called out his warriors if his own village were in danger, but he could see no advantage in leading them off several hundred miles to fight for Nez Perce lands, leaving 1,000 or more women and children unprotected.

The white settlers in the Columbia Basin were too frightened to take an objective look at the situation. They were inclined to give Chief Moses a great deal of credit for his efforts in preventing a widespread war, although he really had done nothing but sit. His delay in acting soon solved the problem for him. After a few weeks the hostile Nez Perce retreated eastward across the Lolo Trail into Montana, and the war scare in the Columbia Basin gradually died out.

The following year, 1878, the Columbia Basin settlers had another great war scare when Chief Buffalo Horn led his Bannock on the warpath through southern Idaho and into eastern Oregon. The whites expected a war party of at least 700 to turn north and cross the Columbia into the Yakima country, gaining many recruits along the way from the Umatilla and Yakima. Then Smoholla and Moses were expected to join with all their forces making a formidable force of perhaps 2,000 men.

Some of the hostile Indians did indeed cross the Columbia, but only in small parties, fugitives from the war

Chief Moses of the Mid-Columbia Salish.
(Eastern Washington State Historical Society)

on their way to safe hiding places. When the whole fighting force collapsed and none of the Columbia River bands had given any help to the war, Chief Moses was given much credit for the result. He did nothing to dispel the notion that he had indeed restrained many of the Indians who otherwise would have gone to war.

Following the Nez Perce War and the troubles of 1878, a reservation was laid out for Moses and his tribe west of the Okanogan River. They moved to this new reservation in 1880, but two years later they were forced to give up all their holdings and move east to the Colville Reservation—a large mountainous tract bounded by the Okanogan, the Columbia, and Canada. They shared this reservation with another Salish tribe, the Sanpoil.

When Chief Joseph and the last of the Nez Perce captives were finally returned to the Northwest in 1885, they were also placed on the Colville Reservation, most of them near the agency at Nespelem, and were put under the supervision of Chief Moses. At first Moses liked this, for he and Joseph had been rather friendly before the war. Later Moses became annoyed because Joseph was held in greater esteem by most of the whites and received more and better publicity in the nation's newspapers.

Chief Joseph had much better manners and the more pleasing personality of the two. In addition, he seems to have been abler as a diplomat and statesman, while Moses' superior reputation as a warrior was of little

172

value in reservation life. Joseph also had a wider acceptance among the Indians of the neighboring tribes. Joseph was taken east, as was Moses, but here again Joseph received more acclaim. Until the death of Moses, in 1899, the two sparred for position and favorable publicity, but they remained friendly to the last. Joseph died in 1904 at Nespelem, Washington.

26 Breaking Up the Indian Reservation

By 1880 DEMANDS for reforms in the treatment of Indians had built up to the point where members of Congress began to take notice. Most of the reform groups supported some sort of program which would change the wild Indian hunter into a tame farmer. The reformers believed that most Indians would take a real interest in settling down and raising crops if each man owned outright a tract of land, instead of working a portion of the tribal holdings.

By law each tribe held the entire reservation in joint ownership. This had been the Indian concept before the white man came, and the various tribes insisted that the communal ownership clause be written into the treaties. To give each Indian his own portion of the tribal lands would require a change in the law. For a long time Congress ignored the cries of the reformers. Then some people decided that their own communities would not thrive until the Indian lands were put under cultivation by white farmers. They knew they had little chance of cutting the size of reservations. Instead, they began to back the request for allotments of land to the individual Indians, knowing that when such a program was finished, there would be millions of acres of land open to white settlement.

Another potent argument which pleased both the local white population and the reformers was that once the Indian owned his farm, he would have to pay local taxes on it. Reservation lands could not be taxed by any local authority.

Even some of the most stubborn Senators who would not even discuss measures for the benefit of the Indians could see some sense in these new arguments. Here was a way to deprive the red man of most of his holdings with a show of legality, giving in with seeming reluctance to the demands of the reformers. In 1887 Congress finally passed the law known as the Dawes Act or the General Allotment Act. Soon the effects of the new law were felt by all the tribes owning good potential farmland near settled country.

The Nez Perce Reservation in central Idaho was one of the first to be put under the allotment program; it offers a good example of the working of the act. The tribe held more than 300 acres of fairly good land for

175

each man, woman, and child—much more land than any farmer of that time could use properly. And yet these Indians were not interested in farming more than little garden plots. They preferred to raise stock, which they could do profitably on their tribal lands, but both the local people and the Indian Bureau officials were opposed to such a program. The initial problem, then, was to get tribal consent to the change which most of the tribesmen did not want.

Finally, a group of twelve tribal representatives and a like number of government officials reached an agreement: The land would be divided, and each Nez Perce receive 80 acres. Then came the knotty question of just who was a Nez Perce and so entitled to his land. The answer was difficult to determine, for the Nez Perce had been intermarrying with other tribes for a century or more and with the whites for seventy-five years.

According to the U.S. Census Bureau, an Indian was anyone having Indian blood to such a degree as to be recognized in his community as an Indian.

According to the Indian Bureau, a man could claim a portion of tribal lands if he was accepted by the tribe as a member or if he had inherited directly from a tribal member. Among the Nez Perce this ruling would give land to several men and women from other tribes who had settled among them.

The Nez Perce themselves accepted as a member of the tribe any person living in the tribe and having one-fourth or more Nez Perce blood. They had dropped from the tribal rolls some Indians with one-fourth to one-half Nez Perce blood, but who lived away from the reservation, often on some other Indian reservation. Persons with one-half or more Nez Perce blood were considered tribal members no matter where they lived, unless such a person chose to claim membership in some other tribe.

It was important that each person with some Indian blood be required to prove the Nez Perce relationship if he expected a share of the land. This applied especially to mixed white and Indian persons. Another group needing careful screening consisted of those who were part Nez Perce and part some other tribe, suct as Umatilla, Yakima, or Flathead. Such persons had to choose formally one or the other of the tribes and be registered there. This would insure that each would receive his share in the treaty benefits but would not get two shares of one in each tribe.

Alice Fletcher, a trained anthropologist, was sent from Washington to make an accurate census, listing each person entitled to a land allotment and checking carefully against double listings, ineligibles, and frauds. All this took a good deal of time and considerable skill. A Nez Perce might have his name in Shahaptin, with variant spellings, or his Indian name might be translated into English, or a regular American name might have been given to him if he had been baptized. Not only might a man be known by all three of these names, he might also have one or two other Indian names from his earlier life.

In addition to all this, a typical Nez Perce family might have one or more children living with them who, in white society, would be listed as orphans living in a foster home, but among the Nez Perce these children of other parents would be accepted as members of the family, on the same footing as the natural offspring of the father and mother.

Hence in completing her rolls, Miss Fletcher had to list the various names of the father and of the mother of each person, his brothers and sisters, and offspring, if any. Also she had to list all the one-half Nez Perce living in other tribes, so each might choose where he would claim treaty benefits.

In addition to all this, the rolls had to list all the Nez Perce war captives who were still being held on the Colville Reservation. None of them was permitted to own a land allotment in Idaho, because they were not allowed to leave the Colville Reservation. What little benefits they might have claimed had been declared forfeited when they went to war.

As soon as the rolls were complete, Miss Fletcher went from place to place on the reservation, supervising while each adult chose his 80 acres; parents chose for their children. Family holdings were usually in one tract and near the village to which the person belonged. Then each allotment was surveyed, and the corners were marked. A total of 2,278 individual allotments were made, coming to 182,240 acres. In addition, the

A contemporary scene of Yakima at the big drum for dancing at White Swan.

(Geoffrey Hilton, Lillah, Washington)

tribe kept 30,000 acres of pasture and timber in common ownership. The chiefs asked that the tribe be allowed to keep all the unalloted land, rather than sell the 542,000 acres to the government, but the officials would not permit this. Such an action would have blocked the real purpose of the bill, the transfer of Indian land to white settlers.

The Nez Perce received $3 an acre for this extra

land, $1,626,000 in all. From this fund each member of the tribe received an immediate payment of $600. The rest was put into a tribal fund under the supervision of the agency superintendent. Then the reservation was declared abolished, and in 1895 white settlers were permitted to file claims on all the extra land.

Most of the Indian reservations in the West were put through the same process, with only minor variations. Then both officials and reformers found that the Indian problem had not been solved at all. Many of the Indians were unwilling or unable to farm their holdings. Instead, they leased their land to some neighboring white farmer and lived on the meager rent, pieced out by some annual payments under the treaty and wages from occasional jobs.

When a Nez Perce died, by law his land had to be divided equally among all his heirs. He was not allowed to will all a tract to one person. In a few years this system made total confusion of the Nez Perce holdings. An 80-acre farm might be owned by as many as fifty people, the plots being too small to make a division practical. On the other hand, one person might own a small plot in each of fifty widely scattered fields, 1 acre here, ½ acre there, and 2 acres someplace else. He might easily own 80 acres or more, but he had no chance to farm any of it.

Some of the confusion ended when the individual Indians were given permission to sell their lands, but few of the other Indians could buy out their relatives.

As a result, some white man stepped in and bought up all the holdings in a tract. Even today some of the Nez Perce lands are still held in these multiple small parcels. All this helps explain why there are few Nez Perce farmers today.

27 Changes in Indian Culture

ONCE THE INDIAN WARS had ended and the tribesmen had been placed securely on reservations, the vast majority of Americans no longer feared them— and so ceased to hate them. Instead, the Indians, especially the dashing mounted warriors of the Plains, gradually became interesting, romantic figures. "Buffalo Bill" Cody and others recruited bands of mounted Indians to appear in Wild West shows. Such shows enjoyed a great popularity in the Eastern United States and Europe.

The wild charge of the braves in full war paint, their eagle-feather headdresses waving in the breeze, their colorful horses rearing and jumping, their war whoops filling the air—all combined to make a colorful spec-

This Yakima girl has been chosen to be a parade queen.
(Geoffrey Hilton)

tacle which appealed greatly to the public imagination. Illustrated magazines also featured the fighters in their warbonnets, and prints of the famous painting "Custer's Last Stand" were displayed in the windows of hundreds of saloons. In time the image of the mounted Indian with his warbonnet replaced the older "Hiawatha" image of the Indian in a canoe, and the ordinary person came to regard the warbonnet as the identifying badge of a real Indian. This impression was strengthened by the Indian head penny, depicting a small girl wearing a small war bonnet.

Today many visitors to the West will not recognize a person as a real Indian if he appears without the feathered headdress. To attract tourists and to stave off endless repetitions of the same old question, this badge of the Indian is sometimes worn by a totem pole carver on the Pacific coast and by a Navaho woman rug weaver on the brink of the Grand Canyon.

The popularity of the Wild West shows and a rapidly developing interest in the cowboy led many Western communities to put on Western shows of their own each year. From the first, these shows stressed the riding of bucking horses, roping of steers, and a parade of some kind. Soon the parade committee learned that a large group of mounted Indians in costume added the needed note of color that would attract the tourists.

Pendleton, in northeastern Oregon, was a leader in setting up such a show, called the Pendleton Roundup. Located in good stock country near the Umatilla Reservation, Pendleton could put on quite a show with the local cowboys and Indians. Early photos show that the street parade each year featured a large group of Indian warriors, followed by a group of Indian women, all mounted and in native costume. In addition, the parade included cowboys, stagecoaches, freight wagons with two to four span of horses, and other Western rigs.

To keep the Indians available for the tourists with their cameras at Pendleton, a large campground was laid out near the show grounds where a number of tipis were set up in an old-style camp circle. In a few years the Indians also staged a few dances in the camp, the throb of the big drum and the chants echoing as the braves danced around in the firelight.

The financial success of the Pendleton Roundup soon led many other towns in the Columbia Basin to put on similar shows. Some of these grew large, and in time the roundups at Ellensburg, Washington, and Lewiston, Idaho, ranked just below Pendleton in size and importance. As the number of shows increased, some were called stampedes, frontier days, or rodeos, but in each case the promoters tried to have some Indians in costume and a camp with tipis. This cost money, of course, for the Indians would not do all this for nothing. Some of them made a little extra money by posing for pictures.

The Indians liked the excitement of the shows and the attention they received. Naturally they wanted to please the promoters and the crowds. Each year they

185

showed up in more colorful and elaborate costumes, borrowing ideas liberally first from the circuses and later from the movies. Brilliant modern dyes, sequins, spangles, and even ostrich plumes were used.

In the Wild West shows the Indians often worked with cavalrymen. From these they borrowed the cavalry gauntlet and, from the cowboy, the vest. (About 1900 in warm weather cowboys wore unbuttoned vests as their outer garment.) The Indians decorated both the vest and the gauntlets with beadwork. About this time they discarded the colorful store shirt, so popular in the 1880's, and returned to the loose buckskin shirt with beadwork trim. Leggings of cloth gave way to buckskin trousers, and the breechclout to a small beaded apron. Roaches, once so popular among the Nez Perce, were replaced with the warbonnet.

Among the women the first item of the old culture to go was the neat, attractive basket hat. This was replaced by the silk kerchief, which in turn gave way to the beaded crown, considered more appropriate for the queens and princesses of the special events. Beading on the dresses became more elaborate until a woman's costume might weigh 20 pounds. In recent years a few of the old basket hats have been worn; some new ones, solidly beaded over the entire outer surface, appear on occasion. The bucksin dresses are now of white, unsmoked skin and are sometimes even fitted, whereas the old-style garments hung loose unless held in by a belt.

Gift of the Gods, Indian translation of *Wah-nee-ta,* is apt description of modern luxury resort established by the Warm Springs Indians on site of old Indian camping grounds.

(W. W. Marsh)

Modern ideas have also brought several changes in dances and dance costumes. The early dances were ceremonial, with simple shuffling steps and accompanying songs. Most of those dances have been lost. In the early days, before the coming of the white man, the big ceremonial dance of the year celebrated the coming of the salmon run. Some tribes also celebrated the first plants of spring with a dance of "first eating." Another time for a big dance was in February, although there seems to be no explanation of how the date was set. For the last 100 years or more the Nez Perce have chosen Washington's Birthday for their mid-winter dance.

The difficulty in determining more details about the old dances arises from the tendency of the Columbia Basin tribes, particularly the Nez Perce, to borrow. No sooner had these Western tribes met the Crows in the buffalo country than they began borrowing all sorts of items, including dances. The first Crow dance to reach the Nez Perce became so popular that it replaced older dances in a few years.

During the Depression of the 1930's, agency super-intendents encouraged dancing among the tribes to keep up their spirits and fill their spare time.

By this time many of the young people were attending the public high schools, where they learned social dancing by couples. This led the girls to ask for some couple dancing at the Indian affairs. They were given the rabbit dance, with partners clasping hands and circling the floor. Then came the owl dance and variations until by 1967 at least a third of the evening was spent in couple dances, and the women danced only once by themselves.

Following World War II, public interest in the dances increased rapidly, and the various tribes responded by staging more dances. These affairs are scheduled, staged, and managed entirely by the Indians, although white spectators are welcome, and a few whites who have appropriate costumes and have learned the steps are permitted to dance if they wish. The dances are staged in Indian communities such as Nespelem, Wapato, White Swan, Toppenish, Lapwai, Kamiah, and Ronan. The dates are arranged so there will be no conflict, and dancers can make the entire circuit if jobs do not interfere.

Visiting Indians often attend from other areas and come dressed in their own different costumes. Often a dance group comes from the coast of British Columbia, dresses in coast costumes, and puts on a special dance from their culture. Crows and Blackfeet come in from Montana, and once in a while a Sioux or a Cheyenne appears.

In these large dances the music is from a big drum, as much as seven feet in diameter, and with only one head. The drum is placed flat on the floor or ground, with five to nine expert drummers around it, a drumstick in each hand. The men beat in unison and chant as they beat. Sometimes a few extra men may help in the chanting and take their turns with the drum. It is considered an honor for a visitor to be invited to take his place at the drum.

As interest in dancing grew, the costumes became more colorful and elaborate, with more feathers and more beadwork. A man often started with a close-

189

fitting dyed suit of long underwear and added feather rosettes on each shoulder, a big dance bustle behind, a beaded apron in front, a beaded collar and tie around his neck, a circlet of sleigh bells around each ankle, and, of course, a warbonnet on his head.

One of the fine older dances, the feather dance, has been lost. In this a ranking war leader or chief cleared the dance circle and ceremoniously deposited a small, fluffy eagle feather in the center. Then on cue from the drummers, any warrior who had taken scalps in combat might come forward and pick up the feather. The Indians have agreed that the coup must have been won in some fight between tribal forces and an enemy, either Indian or white. Equally brave deeds by an Indian soldier in the U.S. armed forces do not qualify a man, or there would be hundreds from World Wars I and II and the Korean War.

The last feather dance among the Nez Perce was staged a few years ago for the last surviving fighter of the Nez Perce War. The old warrior was ninety-three at the time, and the crowd watched in hushed admiration as he went through the historic ritual.

Any well-behaved visitor is welcome at any of the dances if he can find room to get in. He will find color and excitement. When the young men step out in their classic dance, the big drum booming under the impact of six or seven blows struck in unison and the voices of the drummers raised in the old chant, the visitor recaptures briefly some of the feeling of a bygone age.

190

28 The Indian Reorganization Act of 1934

IN THE 1920's the Bureau of Indian Affairs came under bitter attacks by several of the tribes and their influential white friends. Although there was no graft scandal concerning the handling of tribal funds and the agency employees operated strictly within the law, the Indians believed they were being oppressed and and their funds were being spent with little attention to the needs of the tribesmen.

Tribal funds went for the agency payroll, with most of the employees white men who had a great deal of authority over their charges. Agency superintendents living in government housing used tribal funds to refurbish and remodel their houses, sometimes each year. The Indians and their friends insisted that such items of expense should be borne by the government while all tribal funds should be spent directly on the tribe and its members.

Then, too, only those Indians subservient to the superintendent in charge of the funds could hope to receive their share of tribal money without a good deal of red tape and extra hindrances. In this way the more ambitious Indians who might accomplish a great deal and in time develop into tribal leaders were ignored or even subjected to petty restrictions. Such Indians often left the tribe and went out on their own.

Especially irksome to the Indians was the continuing pressure from the agency to break down all vestiges of tribal unity and eliminate any of the old religious rites. This was a precautionary measure to forestall another possible Ghost Dance type of rebellion. Indians were forced to cut off their long hair and to give up their warhorses. In addition, there was a federal law—a sedition act—forbidding Indians from one reservation to communicate with those on another reservation unless the messages went through government channels.

The agents were ably assisted in these efforts by the various mission workers and church groups. Boarding schools were set up so small children could be taken from their parents for long periods of time and thus break down the strong family groups found throughout the Columbia Basin.

Finally, the various reform groups managed to get a hearing in Washington. The Indians were included in the New Deal program of President Franklin D. Roosevelt. As a result, in 1934 Congress passed the Indian Reorganization Act which did away with some of the abuses mentioned. The act encouraged each tribe to set up a tribal government to handle its own affairs. Most of the Great Basin and Plateau tribes voted for tribal government.

The act also put an end to the system of giving allotments of tribal lands to individuals. Instead, such land had to be held in ownership by the whole tribe, although it could be leased to individual tribal members or even to white farmers for short periods. All the land which the government had taken from the tribes and which had not yet been settled by the whites was returned. This amounted to a total of about 50,000,000 acres, much of it rough, wild land, but of some value for grazing, and part of it covered with marketable timber.

Many of the small holdings of white settlers scattered among the tribal lands were bought up by the Indian Bureau with federal funds and deeded to the tribes. The tribes were encouraged to use their own funds to buy up all the small plots owned by many heirs and consolidate these plots into workable holdings. Also, any Indian owning an allotment could put it back under tribal supervision and protection, thus escaping the local property taxes.

The Indian Service was improved by placing all the jobs under civil service regulations, with preference being given to qualified Indians on all appointments. Some vocational training was offered to fit the Indians for such jobs and for employment in the white communities.

The act had an immediate noticeable effect on the tribes in the Columbia Plateau and on several in the Great Basin. It came in the middle of the Depression, when many of the Indians were struggling to stay alive. Seasonal work in the hop fields and the fruit orchards had fallen off. Many an Indian family dug into the family trunks and traded off fine old costumes and heirlooms for potatoes and a little meat. Once the act was passed, the tribes began to organize and to develop their tribal resources, with the new jobs created by these projects going to the Indians.

A leader in the movement was the Flathead tribe of some 3,000 members. They occupied a remnant of their old reservation in western Montana south of Flathead Lake. They were an intelligent group, with some formal education and several good leaders. In 1935 they voted to set up a tribal government, and in a short time they had adopted a constitution and bylaws. A few months later, in 1936, they formed a tribal corporation to conduct their business affairs.

The corporation's chief concern was the proper management of 192,577 acres of tribal lands given back to them that year. Much of the land was fairly good for summer pasture, but the tribe had no stock to put on it. They leased their grasslands to the neighboring ranchmen on a short-term lease. Timber from the tribal holdings was sold to the local lumber mills. The money from these two sources was then used to buy up fractional holdings and small farms on the reservation. Then the Flatheads decided they could do better if they cut their own timber and sawed it in their own mills, thus making more jobs for their men. The success of the Flathead program led other tribes to proceed on the same pattern.

A farming operation, small in acreage, but important to the local Indians, was begun on the Fort McDermitt Reservation in northern Nevada. There the Western Shoshoni and Paiute owned several hundred acres of hayland. They put this land into a corporate farm, and any family wanting to share in the hay crop had to supply some of the labor of putting up the hay. The crop was then divided among the workers according to the amount of time each worked. Thus, with almost no cash expense, this group each year harvested a good crop of hay to be used in wintering their cattle. With adequate winter feed, the cattle herds increased in four years from 200 to 1,200 head.

This project had special significance, for it was planned and conducted by a group of the despised Diggers. Their success demonstrated that ambitious Indians of almost any group could adjust to modern conditions and, with a little encouragement, could handle their own affairs.

These same Western Shoshoni and Paiute also made an important addition to their local court system. To provide for appeals in civil cases, they set up a permanent panel of fifteen respected older tribesmen. Any Indian dissatisfied with a finding by the tribal court in civil action could demand a review by a special board of three chosen from the panel and acceptable to both parties to the suit. The decision of this board was final.

The Colville Reservation in northern Washington is the home of a mixture of Spokane and Sanpoil of Salish stock and some descendants of the Nez Perce war captives. This diverse group had some difficulty in adjusting themselves to a common government, partly because of the friction between the various groups. The Salish complained that the Nez Perce were trying to take over their reservation. In 1935, when the tribes were given the right to local government, the Indian Bureau extended their supervision over this reservation for ten more years. By 1939, encouraged by their supervisors, the Indians put all their tribal timberlands on a sustained yield basis, cutting the mature trees at a steady annual rate. Under this plan the local sawmills could depend on a steady, adequate supply of logs each year and would not be forced to move the mills because all the timber had been cut off. This security for the mills offers some job security for the workers and allows each to establish a permanent home and become a part of a stable community. The success of this program on the Colville Reservation helped persuade other tribes to adopt sustained-yield programs of their own, thus obtaining more profits from the timber, besides providing steady employment.

196

29 Protection of Treaty Rights

FOR MANY YEARS the Indian tribes suffered from numerous violations of their treaty rights, guaranteed them by the federal government. Some of the troubles stemmed from the actions of private citizens, but others came from action by government officials. Usually when a person or a group has suffered a loss through the unlawful actions of another, the remedy is to sue for damages in the proper lawcourt, but no person or group may sue the United States government without express permission from Congress.

When the Shoshoni on the Wind River Reservation in central Wyoming were permitted to bring such a suit, they secured a large sum in damages in 1935. The success of this suit stirred up several other tribes with like grievances. Under their new tribal status and with tribal funds at their disposal, many of the tribal councils began preparing for such suits. Congress decided it would be better to have these special problems handled by a special commission rather than dump this extra load on the overworked federal courts.

In 1946 Congress passed the Indian Claims Commission Act, setting up a special commission for the express purpose of hearing the Indians' claims. A decision by the commission would have the same standing as a fededal court decision and could be appealed. The commission was expected to give most of its time and attention to various land problems arising under the many treaties. It would consider questions such as the following:

Had tribal lands been taken unlawfully? Had tribal lands been bought by the federal government for less than their market value at the time of purchase? Had resources from tribal lands been taken unlawfully by intruders while the lands were specifically under government protection?

An important early case was that of the Ute. They had lost 11,000,000 acres of land following the White River trouble. By the time the Shoshoni had won their case in 1935 it was known that the former Ute lands contained very valuable deposits of coal, shale oil, and uranium. The Ute began pressing their claims for damages.

Once the Indian Claims Commission had been set up,

the Ute were on hand, ready to present their evidence. Within four years the claim was settled in the tribe's favor. The Indians were awarded a total of $31,700,000 damages. This success astounded the other tribes and encouraged them to bring claims of their own.

For years the Nez Perce had believed that they had claims just as valid as those of the Ute. Now they studied the new law, trying to determine the best method to follow. At length they had a tribal meeting at Kamiah, Idaho, in March, 1951. About 200 voting members of the tribe were present and, after a lengthy discussion, agreed to hire a law firm and proceed with the claims.

A petition was filed with the commission on July 25, 1951, asking that the Nez Perce tribe be paid additional compensation for the lands ceded under the treaties of 1855 and 1863 and the agreement of 1893. This brought an immediate claim from an opposing group of Nez Perce, those descended from the captives of the Nez Perce War and now living on the Colville Reservation. They claimed to be the true Nez Perce tribe and entitled to all payments due on the claims.

In October, 1952, the commission ruled in favor of the Nez Perce tribal council set up in 1935. The dissenting group then appealed to the United States Court of Claims, which upheld the commission. This decision cleared the way for the suit to continue. At this time the tribal lawyers decided to present all the claims for ceded lands in one group and all claims for trespass damage and the removal of gold in another group. The commission assigned Docket No. 175 to the land claims and Docket No. 180-A to the gold claims.

The office of the U.S. Attorney General filed a blanket denial of all the Indian claims and in effect asked the tribe to offer substantial proof to support their petitions. It was evident that the amount of the award depended on the following items: (1) The exact boundaries of the Nez Perce reservation as established by the Treaty of 1855, thus determining the amount of land ceded in 1863; (2) the true market value of the ceded land on April 17, 1867, the date the Treaty of 1863 was ratified by the Senate; and (3) the value of the gold removed from the reservation from the time gold was discovered in August, 1860, until April 17, 1867, when the Nez Perce ceded all their gold lands.

In the Treaty of 1855 the Nez Perce accepted a reservation with boundaries which were clearly understood by them. Governor Stevens had these boundaries written into the treaty, but it appears that the clerk who wrote them down was a little careless. At the time this did not seem to be a matter of any special importance, for both the Nez Perce and Governor Stevens expected the boundaries would soon be surveyed and marked, as terms of the treaty provided, and with the guidance of the tribal leaders. However, these boundaries were never surveyed or marked.

Once the Nez Perce had been coerced into signing away almost all their land in the Treaty of 1863, they had no further interest in showing anyone where the old boundaries had been set. The various Army officers and Indian agents assigned to Fort Lapwai were not interested either. Hence, when the tribe tried in 1952 to establish the amount of land put into their reservation in 1855, they had no definite lines or markers to work from, and all the signers of the treaties had died long ago. The historian hired by the tribe to help with the case was given the task of correlating any maps of the area made by members of Governor Stevens' party with modern maps of the same area and to allocate place-names mentioned in the treaty to the proper natural features.

At the time he negotiated the Treaty of 1855, Governor Stevens also had the task of surveying possible routes for a transcontinental railroad from Minnesota to the Pacific coast. He and his helpers had no reason to separate their notes and materials on the Indian affairs from their railway survey. As a result, all their reports, journals, and maps were printed in twelve massive volumes under the title *Pacific Railway Survey Reports.* Here, often well buried in a mass of other material, were important items concerning the Nez Perce lands.

One item concerning the northern boundary of the original reservation will illustrate the value of the survey records in the Nez Perce law case. A comparison of the daily journals with the record of distance traveled each day proved that Stevens considered the present main stream of the Palouse River to be the South Fork of the Palouse mentioned in the treaty. Since this stream was

201

designated in the treaty as the northern boundary of the reservation, the proving of this one point added 667,000 acres of farmland with an 1867 value of about $650,000 to the Nez Perce Reservation.

The exact location of the southeastern corner of the reservation could not be established until after the point had been compromised by mutual agreement by the lawyers for the tribe and for the government. As a result, the tribe lost its claim to a large amount of land and several important gold-producing areas.

As the land claim developed, the tribe hired a competent appraiser. He was to place an estimated value on each section of land involved, considering the kind of land, the market price of such land in the area in 1867, and the location of each parcel of land with respect to the transportation available at that time. Mining specialists were trained to give an estimate of the value of the gold taken from the reservation up to April 17, 1867.

How is it possible to arrive at some reasonable figure for the amount of gold dug after a lapse of ninety years? Then how do you determine a reasonable figure to cover the cost of the actual mining? The stampede to the Nez Perce diggings started in the spring of 1861, just as the Civil War began. Thousands of men from all over the country, many of them from the border states, and a goodly number of foreigners came rushing into the Columbia Basin. They were anxious to find gold and as anxious to avoid going to war. When they left the mining camps, they made little effort to give an accounting of their activities or an estimate of their gold hoard.

202

Floaters from related activities also had no reason to report their earnings. And much of the gold mined had been spent in camp for supplies and recreation.

With only rugged mountain trails entering the Nez Perce gold country from the south, east, and north, most of the traffic to and from the camps, of necessity, followed the Columbia River, and gold miners outward-bound with their take usually went through Portland. For the early period, 1861 to midsummer, 1863, the Nez Perce mines produced almost every ounce of gold passing through the city. This situation changed drastically after July, 1863, when several rich new strikes were made on the John Day and Powder rivers in eastern Oregon and on the Boise in southern Idaho. Hence, any figures on gold shipments through Portland from August, 1863 to April, 1867, are of little value in determining the output of the Nez Perce mines.

The firm of Tracy and Company handled most of the gold down the Columbia until May, 1862, when Wells, Fargo and Company absorbed both the firm and its carrying trade. Then could the shipping records of Wells, Fargo be used? No, for they had all been burned in the San Francisco fire of 1906. This left only the local column of the Portland *Oregonian,* which each week carried an account of steamboats arriving from up the Columbia. The reporter estimated the amount of gold carried by all express messengers and by the private passengers. Although this record is admittedly incomplete, it does give some basis for an estimate.

In the Nez Perce claims case, with both groups using

the same source material, experts from the tribe arrived at a total of $25,913,000, while equally competent men on the government side decided the figure should be $15,133,780.

An equally complex problem was presented in determining the true market value of the land as of April 17, 1867. Each section of land in the vast area had to be evaluated in regard to type of land, kind of soil, best possible use, and the like. Then a value per acre for each kind of soil had to be assigned for 1867, taking into consideration the kind of land being bought in that particular area at that time and the prices paid. Some allowance had to be made for very good land too far from any road to be desirable in 1867.

During the period this work was in progress, the historian had to be on call when any of the law firms or the appraisers needed information of any sort from the old records. The questions were numerous and varied. Are the Moh-ha-na-she and the Wo-na-ne-she two different streams or variant spellings for the same stream? What is the present name for this stream? What was cordwood worth at Lapwai in 1861? How much did the sawing cost? The questions were innumerable.

After all this work was finished, the result was turned over to the Indian Claims Commission for a long and involved discussion concerning the relative worth of certain reports and the weight to be given each when two or more reports on the same item did not agree on details. Finally, the commission arrived at a total of

$20,000,000 as the value of the gold taken from the reservation lands. In spite of the lengthy deliberations, an outsider might be forgiven for concluding that the commission actually took an approximate average of the two estimates, $25,913,611 and $15,133,780, then tailored its decisions on the various items to fit.

An equally long and involved discussion of probable mining costs followed, with the commission finally deciding that the miners probably averaged a net profit of 30 percent or $6,000,000, and the Nez Perce tribe was entitled to a royalty of one-half the profit, $3,000,-000.

The two sets of appraisers differed more widely in assessing the land than in determining the amount of gold. The estimate for the tribe, $18,250,000 for 6,932,-270 acres, averaged $2.63 an acre, whereas the government appraisers set a figure of $400,000, or 6 cents an acre. The commission finally settled on a figure of $4,-650,000, about 67 cents an acre. All the totals in both cases were included in the findings of the commission handed down on December 31, 1959.

Other claims from various tribes followed the same general course, and each took several years for a decision to be reached. The Nez Perce case is given in such detail because it is a good example of a land case, the records being fairly complete. A study of this case shows that it is much easier to say, "Pay the Indian for his land," than it is to determine what land and how much to pay. Although the process of handling the Indian claims may seem long and involved, keep in mind that public funds are involved, and the whole process must stand up under close scrutiny by guardians of the treasury, as well as by people unfriendly toward the whole idea.

30 The Spending of Tribal Funds

IN THE 1950's the Ute and several tribes in the Columbia Basin became quite wealthy, as Indian tribes go, with each tribal council having several million dollars in the treasury. The flow of large sums to the tribes did not depend entirely on the settlement of ancient claims by long-drawn-out lawsuits.

After World War II, when the federal government decided to build a huge hydroelectric plant on the Columbia at The Dalles, they first were careful to settle all the Indian claims concerning the riverbanks to be flooded by the new project. A few miles upstream from the damsite was Celilo Falls, the finest salmon-fishing grounds in the whole Columbia River system. Here several of the tribes had caught their yearly supply of fish for the last several thousand years.

In a series of meetings with tribal representatives, the cash value of the fishing rights was determined. Then this sum was apportioned to the various tribes with valid claims, with the Yakima getting the largest payment. Next came the Warm Springs group and the Nez Perce, with a few million each. The money was paid as soon as Congress passed the necessary appropriation bill.

The sudden wealth from land claims, gold claims, and fishing rights, all within a few years, presented the tribal councils with the problem of the best use of the funds. Of course, the individual Indians wanted all the cash right away, to be given out on a per capita basis as fast as the payments came in from Washington. A large part of each payment was distributed in this way, usually spread over several months rather than in one lump sum. The Indians responded to this sudden acquisition of easy money just as any other ordinary group of Americans would do. They went on a shopping spree each payment day and soon were broke, but it was fun while it lasted.

The Bureau of Indian Affairs, by various means, persuaded the tribes to put a substantial portion of the funds into long-range plans for lasting benefits. Individual Indians who owned houses could ask for and usually receive enough money to install indoor plumbing, with a drilled well and an electric pump to supply the water for isolated homes. Then the Rural Electrification Agency helped bring electric lines to the homes. This encouraged the Indians to buy electric stoves, washers, and refrigerators and to repair, paint, and paper the interiors. But even then there are many Indian families who can see no reason to go to the expense and bother of painting the exterior. Thus, a passerby may see in the Indian communities many weather-beaten houses with electric and telephone service, large TV antennas, and shiny autos parked in the driveways.

The close-knit Nez Perce group at Kamiah decided their young people needed a good community center for all sorts of club and group meetings, social affairs, winter dances, and, above all, a good athletic program. The tribe owned a good hall at Lapwai, inherited from the old agency, but Kamiah had nothing. The local leaders used tribal funds to plan and build a fine center with a good athletic plant, a lounge and snack bar, a restaurant, and some offices. The building is surrounded by a large paved parking lot to hold the many autos which bring the modern Nez Perce to the "old-time" affairs which attempt to preserve some aspects of the old culture.

This building at Kamiah, planned, built, and managed by the Nez Perce with Nez Perce funds, is an object of pride to the Indians. Their young people have a finer plant and a more comprehensive program of activities than is available to the white teen-agers of the town. Whites are welcome to the building as spectators to the athletic events and the winter dances, and tourists are encouraged by highway signs to eat at the snack bar and the restaurant. If special notice is given, a group will be served with old-time Nez Perce foods, prepared by trained cooks in a modern kitchen. Although the resulting dishes contain ingredients unfamiliar to most people, there is nothing put in which should bother even a squeamish stomach.

The Nez Perce are now proposing to use some of the tribal grazing lands for a large stock ranch run by Nez Perce employees. There they expect to breed, raise, and train horses to sell for pleasure riding. Emphasis will be placed on the Appaloosa breed, the spotted horse which has such a secure place in Nez Perce history.

The Nez Perce council takes a deep interest in better education for the young people of the tribe. The thirst for learning which sent the delegation to St. Louis in 1831 and furnished more than 200 students for the Spalding school in 1837 has never been satisfied. Early in this century, when few white youths of the Columbia Basin ever went beyond the eighth grade, Nez Perce students were being graduated from the Indian school at Carlyle, Pennsylvania. One outstanding Nez Perce scholar, Dr. Archie Phinney, earned his doctorate at Columbia University in 1930. Quite a few of the tribe have advanced degrees in several fields, and several more finish college each year—all this from a total population of about 2,500. The tribal council has a program of scholarships and grants to encourage their more gifted young people to get a higher education, and it has produced results.

Quite a few of the Nez Perce learn trades. The young men find several job opportunities near their homes. Some of them work for the federal and state forestry services and for the state highway department. Others go into logging, lumbering, trucking, and farming. Several of the girls choose nursing as a career. So far there has been no serious unemployment problem in this tribe in recent years.

Other tribal councils trying to emulate the Nez Perce have been less successful with their programs for the young people. The Yakima built longhouses at White Swan, Wapato, and Toppenish, but they are not as fine as the hall at Kamiah or as well run. The council has talked for years of building a good motel and a museum near the highway just east of Union Gap, a good spot for such a development, but it has not yet reached the serious planning stage.

For some reason the young people from the other tribes accomplish less in advanced study than do the Nez Perce. Few of them are graduated from college, and those with less education have difficulty in getting and holding permanent jobs. Usually there is work in the summer and much unemployment in the winter. A great many of them work as agricultural laborers each summer, in the sugar beet fields, fruit orchards, and hop farms.

Although the Warm Springs young people have not done as well in advanced schooling as they might, the tribal council has a positive program to provide permanent employment for many of them in tribally owned businesses. Their first project created a good deal of interest in the Northwest.

Warm Springs Reservation takes its name from a large

211

spring at the bottom of a rugged canyon putting out water at 140 degrees. There in the desert country the sun shines 345 days a year, but the nights are cool, even in midsummer. The springs are just across the Cascade Range from 1,000,000 people living in the metropolitan area of Portland and only 80 miles from the city center. Two good highways, U.S. 26 and U.S. 97, intersect a few miles to the southwest of the springs, offering easy access for tourists.

When the tribal council looked around for a desirable investment for tribal funds, one which would return a reasonable profit and would furnish steady jobs for the young people, it concluded that the Warm Springs canyon was an excellent place for a resort and playground for visitors. Soon plans were drawn up for an elaborate development, to be constructed in several stages.

On Labor Day, 1963, work was begun on the first group of structures, a hotel, a lodge, a trailer court, a sauna, a hot pool at 123 degrees, a large swimming pool at 80 degrees, and a wading pool. If visitors preferred a touch of the old days, they might rent genuine tipis for sleeping quarters instead of taking a room at the lodge or hotel. A string of range horses, Indian-raised and trained, waited to carry people on trail rides. About thirty young Indian men and women staffed the complex, with some trained white personnel for the management.

The first section of the resort, Kah-nee-ta, was opened on Memorial Day, 1964, with a salmon feast, Indian dancing, and plenty of publicity. The steady flow of customers has made this a sound business venture and has encouraged further expansion, including a restaurant, a golf course, and a section ready for people who would like to build retirement homes in the canyon.

The Warm Springs Indians own large holdings of ponderosa pine forests, which can produce 100,000,000 board feet of lumber a year on a sustained-yield program of cutting. If the tribe logged, hauled, and processed its own timber, instead of selling the standing timber to neighboring sawmills, it could provide jobs for about 250 men, which is close to the total of the able-bodied adult males available on the reservation. Such an operation would require an investment of about $12,700,000, which could be obtained from the tribal funds and federal loans.

Although this lumbering complex has been carefully planned by competent engineers and has been approved by a vote of the tribe, it is being strongly opposed by the lumbermen and businessmen of the nearby town of Madras. They would suffer if the logs went to new mills on the reservation, instead of to the mills now operating at Madras. This project was all set to go in 1967, but the opposition, combined with a shortage of federal funds, has prevented any further action. Meanwhile, the tribe continues to collect for its trees.

31 Will the Tribes Vanish?

THE COMBINED TOTAL of all the Indian tribes in the Great Basin and Plateau area is about 22,000 people. In contrast, the white population in the same area is about 2,500,000. Hence, the Indians are out-numbered more than 100 to 1 and go unnoticed except in a few villages and towns where they have solid groups and are able to retain a vestige of the old culture. Some of the towns with a significant percentage of Indians in each are Wapato and Toppenish in Washington; Lapwai, Kamiah, and Desmet in Idaho; and Ronan in Montana.

In addition, there are the reservations where the Indians are the dominant group. These are Warm Springs and Umatilla in Oregon; Colville and Spokane in Washington; Coeur d'Alene and Fort Hall in Idaho; Duck

Valley, Pyramid Lake, and Walker River in Nevada; and Uinta and Ouray (one reservation) in Utah.

There are three significant reasons why these Indians as tribal groups have few outstanding accomplishments to their credit in the last half century. The first is their relatively small numbers. In most communities the scattered Indian families have become just a part of the general population, taking their places in local society as individuals. This is, on the whole, a satisfactory development, but any contributions from these people are attributed to the individual, rather than to his tribe.

Second, the Indians on the reservations lack leaders. The intelligent and ambitious young people are encouraged by scholarships and grants from the tribal funds to go off to college or to a city and learn a trade. Many of them volunteer or are drafted for the armed services and get job training there. After these people have received their training and have had a look at the world outside the reservation, they seldom come back to live. They can find better jobs and better living conditions outside. As a result, they are lost to the tribe as potential tribal leaders.

Third is the benevolent and protective Bureau of Indian Affairs. The bureau and its personnel are dedicated in principle to making the Indians self-sufficient as quickly as possible. Several fine plans have been developed to achieve this goal. But the better these plans work, the sooner the bureau will find itself with no useful work to do.

215

An important innovation in 1968 was to invite the tribal leaders to the area meeting to help formulate new plans for the future. These Indians were asked to offer some of their ideas for the betterment of the tribes.

At this time the Indians of the Great Basin and the Plateau areas are slowly being absorbed into the general population, through intermarriage with the whites, as well as through families leaving the reservations for better jobs. The Bureau of Indian Affairs is actively trying to counteract the trend and hopes to retain the tribal organizations and some of the old culture. The bureau is more successful with the smaller, remoter groups. Some of these will probably remain under bureau control with little change for several years.

Selected Bibliography

BAILEY, PAUL, *Wovoka, the Indian Messiah.* Los Angeles, Westernlore Press, 1957.

BRIMLOW, GEORGE F., *The Bannock Indian War of 1878.* Caldwell, Ida., Caxton, 1938.

BROWN, MARK H., *The Flight of the Nez Perce.* New York, Putnam, 1966.

COX, ROSS, *The Columbia River.* Norman, University of Oklahoma Press, 1957.

DRURY, E. M., *Henry Harmon Spalding.* Caldwell, Ida., Caxton, 1936.

———, *Marcus Whitman, M.D.* Caldwell, Ida., Caxton, 1937.

HAINES, FRANCIS, *The Nez Perces.* Norman, University of Oklahoma Press, 1955.

HEBARD, GRACE RAYMOND, *Sacajawea.* Glendale, Calif., Arthur H. Clark, 1957.

IRVING, WASHINGTON, *Adventures of Captain Bonneville,* any ed.

JESSETT, THOMAS E., *Chief Spokane Gary.* Minneapolis, Denison, 1960.

The Journals of Lewis and Clark, Bernard DeVoto, ed., Boston, Houghton, Mifflin, 1953.

KIP, LAWRENCE, *Army Life on the Pacific.* New York, 1859.

———, *The Indian Council in the Valley of the Walla Walla, 1855.* Printed, not published, San Francisco, 1855.

MADSEN, BRIGHAM D., *The Bannocks of Idaho.* Caldwell, Ida., Caxton, 1958.

MANRING, BENJAMIN, *The Conquest of the Coeur d'Alenes, Spokanes and Palouses.* Spokane, 1912.

McWHORTER, L. V., *Yellow Wolf.* Caldwell, Ida., Caxton, 1940.

217

PADEN, IRENE D., *The Wake of the Prairie Schooner.* New York, Macmillan, 1943.

PARKER, SAMUEL, *Journal of an Exploring Tour Beyond the Rocky Mountains.* Ithaca, N.Y. 1838.

RELANDER, CLICK, *Drummers and Dreamers.* Caldwell, Ida., Caxton, 1956.

ROCKWELL, WILSON, *The Utes: A Forgotten People.* Denver, Sage Books, 1956.

ROSS, ALEXANDER, *Fur Hunters of the Far West.* Norman, University of Oklahoma Press, 1956.

RUBY, ROBERT H., and BROWN, JOHN A., *Half-Sun on the Columbia.* Norman, University of Oklahoma Press, 1965.

SPLAWN, A. J., *Kamiakin, the Last Hero of the Yakimas.* Portland, 1917.

SPRAGUE, MARSHALL, *Massacre: The Tragedy at White River.* Boston, Little, Brown, 1957.

TEIT, JAMES A., "The Salishan Tribes of the Western Plateau," 45th *Annual Report.* Washington, Bureau of American Ethnology, 1930.

TRENHOLM, VIRGINIA COLE, and CARLEY, MAURINE, *The Shoshonis: Sentinels to the Rockies.* Norman, University of Oklahoma Press, 1964.

Index

222

The Author

FRANCIS HAINES was reared in the open range country of Montana near the Continental Divide and educated in Montana schools. He received his master's degree from the University of Montana and his doctorate degree in Western United States history from the University of California at Berkeley. Since his retirement from teaching history, he has devoted his full time to writing. He has published many books and articles on Indians of the Columbia Plateau and the Great Basin.